76 -

BREATHING

BREATHING
The ABC's

Carola H. Speads

Sketches by ALBERT ELIA

Photographs by BONNIE FREER

HARPER COLOPHON BOOKS
Harper & Row, Publishers
New York, Hagerstown, San Francisco, London

FIRST EDITION

Designed by Stephanie Krasnow

Library of Congress Cataloging in Publication Data

Speads, Carola H
    Breathing: the ABC's.
    1. Breathing exercises. 2. Respiration.
I. Title.
RA782.S63   613.1'92   77-11537
ISBN: 0-06-013996-X   78 79 80 81 82 10 9 8 7 6 5 4 3 2 1
ISBN: 0-06-090623-5 (PBK)   78 79 80 81 82 10 9 8 7 6 5 4 3 2 1

In memory of
Elsa Gindler,
my extraordinary teacher and friend

Contents

PART II: THE EXPERIMENTS

Acknowledgments

First of all I would like to acknowledge my debt to the many students who over the years gave me their trust and thus the chance to explore breathing work.

I am grateful to Peter Workman for tempting me to write and to Roberta Ashley for helping in the beginning.

Particular thanks to my students and friends, Andora Hodgin and Cathleen McCaffrey, for their close attention to the English of someone foreign-born.

Thanks ever so much to my friend Kimberly, and to the two artists involved in the illustration of this book, Bonnie Freer, who took the pictures, and Albert Elia, who did the sketches.

Also thanks to Elisabeth Jakab, my editor at Harper & Row, for her editorial help.

And last, but not least, thanks to my husband for enabling me to write this book by so gracefully giving up many hours we could have spent together.

He lives most life whoever breathes most air.

—Elizabeth Barrett Browning

Introduction

Years ago during a discussion about breathing, someone said to me, "Do breathing work? Why? Don't we all breathe?" Of course we do. But the *quality* of our breathing is the point in question, *not the fact* that we breathe. The quality of our breathing determines the quality of our lives: Health, moods, energy, creativity—all depend on the oxygen supply provided by our breathing. But the pressures of our modern-day life have created an almost literally breath-less culture. How many of us are really living in a state of inadequate respiration? Even in the so-called healthy person, overtension (hypertension), flabbiness (hypotension), excitement, and worry, as well as temperature changes and air pollution, may provoke shallow, irregular, or forced breathing.

Helping you to become aware of your breathing and teaching you how to have its full support are the aims of this book. Here I will present the basics—the ABC's of breathing work—rather than a compendium of all possible approaches. But just as you can go on to read anything once you have mastered the alphabet, you will find that these ABC's of breathing will enable you consciously to relate to your breathing and to help yourself when in need.

Some of the effects you will become aware of when doing breathing work successfully are an increase in circulation, normalization of tonus (the basic tension existing independent of voluntary action), and clearer thinking with a positive change in mood. With such results, you will know that your breathing has been changed more than superficially.

Breathing work is built upon the premise of the total unity of the human being. Its results prove the interrelation of body, mind, and emotions. Whether your breathing functions satisfactorily or whether it has been disturbed, not only your physical well-being is affected, but you as a total person benefit or suffer. Your breathing determines whether you are at your best or whether you are at a disadvantage. As you progress with your breathing work, you will realize again and again how much you are influenced by any variation in your breathing—positively when it supports you adequately, or negatively when there is interference with the free flow of your breath.

Because interferences with breathing vary as much as individuals do, breathing work has to be geared to individual needs. There is no set routine to be followed. Whatever you do to help your breathing has to fit your very personal condition at the moment. Each of us has unique ways of using breathing well or of disturbing it. To try to help yourself by fixed exercises would be not only boring but also inefficient. An immense variety of approaches are necessary for successful breathing work. They make procedures and results continually new, exciting, and interesting. Since all our activities depend on breath supply, you will acquire not only a mastery of a technique but a mastery of life.

Your breathing needs have to be met in whatever state you are—at rest, in movement, when you feel peaceful, or when you are upset. Working, playing, or sleeping, your breathing should support you adequately. You need breath to perform tasks without becoming worn out, breath to bear up under adversity, and breath to recuperate from strain. If you succeed in letting your breathing adjust itself freely, your body will function properly, your mind will be clear, and your emotions will not overpower you.

Let us examine now what breathing really does. It is the means by which the body eliminates waste gases (among them carbon dioxide) and replenishes itself with fresh gases (among them oxygen), using the blood as carrier to and from the lungs, where the exchange takes place. Therefore the well-being of your entire body depends on, and is influenced by, your breathing.

As an organic process, breathing is self-regulatory, controlled by the involuntary nervous system that safeguards its functioning. How, then, can it be interfered with, and how are we able to disturb it?

The explanation is that breathing, unlike other involuntary functions, is also partially under the influence of the voluntary nervous system; for instance, muscles, tendons, and joints have an influence on it. So do our thoughts and emotions. Any of these factors can and do affect our breathing. Figure 1 shows the manifold interdependences between breathing and various organs of the body. Effects occur in either direction, from the breathing on the organs or from the organs on the breathing. You will now understand the importance the quality of your breathing has for a good state of bodily and emotional well-being.

This book is *not* going to teach you to breathe (you have done this since you were born). It will focus only on breathing malfunctions, those predicaments involving the *quality of your breathing*. And it will deal only with the difficulties of the so-called healthy person, not those caused by disease of the breathing apparatus. (However, sick people can benefit from several of the experiments if they do them under the supervision of a doctor.)

My purpose is to help you experience how your breathing is working at a given moment, to feel whether and in what way it may have been interfered with, and, most important of all, to show you what can be done to let your breathing function adequately again.

A NOTE ON THE HISTORY OF BREATHING WORK

The importance of breathing has been acknowledged throughout the history of mankind. In the East, the care of breathing was always an integral part of the religions of the Tibetans, Indians, Chinese, and Japanese. It was a feature of the cults of the ancient Egyptians. The ancient Hebrews used the word *wind*, the breath, in context with *soul*. The Bible emphasizes that God, creating Adam, "breathed into his nostrils the breath of life; and man became a living soul." This double meaning of "breathing" extends into modern English usage. The Latin verb *spirare*—to breathe—is used concerning breathing in the words *respiration*—our continuous breathing; *expiration*—our last breath; and in the other sense, concerning our souls

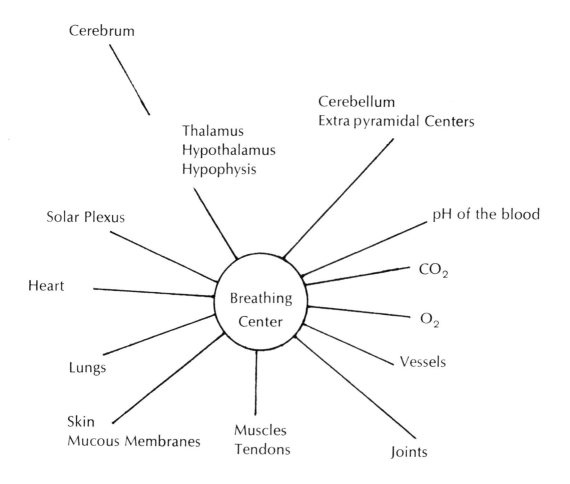

Figure 1. Schematic presentation of stimuli to and from the breathing center. From Methodik der Entspannungs- und Atmungstherapie, by Erna Pasch. Copyright © 1970 by Johann Ambrosius Barth. Reprinted with permission of Johann Ambrosius Barth, Leipzig.

and minds, it is contained in the words *spirit* and *inspiration*. The ancient Greeks used the word *diaphragm* to indicate the mind, as well as for breathing. The pneuma (breathing) theory dominated both the healing arts and philosophy during the first century A.D. In most religions, chants and spoken prayers (intense exhalations) for the "unordained," and special breathing training for the priests, were and still are the rule. All over the world—in fairy tales, legends, in secret societies—breathing plays a significant role.

In the West, in the second half of the nineteenth century, interest in breathing was renewed through the teaching of François Delsarte in Paris. Delsarte, having lost his singing voice through poor instruction, turned to the exploration of movement. Simultaneously he undertook the study of breathing. Eventually breathing work became an integral part of his system of movement education.

After the Franco-Prussian War of 1870–71, Delsarte's system was brought to the United States by his American student, Steele Mackay. Genevieve Stebbins and other teachers who had studied with Mackay spread the Delsarte method in this country. Stebbins achieved such success that word of her work spread to Europe. The German Hede Kallmeyer heard about it and came to New York to study with Stebbins. She taught Delsarte's method in Germany, eventually evolving her own system.*

Around 1910, Elsa Gindler, one of the most outstanding teachers in the field of physical reeducation (in German, *Gymnastik*), became familiar with Delsarte's work through her studies with Hede Kallmeyer. Breathing work became part of her method as well as of all other systems of physical reeducation from 1900 to the present. It was Elsa Gindler who raised the standard of breathing work. She applied to it the highly original ideas she had developed in her movement work: body awareness as the basis, and experimenting as the procedure, instead of the mechanical approach that was generally followed in breathing work then and is still most often used today.

Delsarte's system was not the only method of breathing work that was

* Anyone interested in exploring the development of the Delsarte System in the United States should refer to Ted Shawn's *Every Little Movement* (New York: M. Witmark and Sons, 1954), which contains an extensive bibliography.

relayed back and forth across the Atlantic. There was a second, no less important, influence on breathing work that passed from the United States to Europe.

The Swiss Leo Kofler, who worked as organist and choirmaster at Saint Paul's Chapel, Trinity Parish, in New York around 1877, developed a system of breathing and voice training. His book, *The Art of Breathing*, was translated into German in 1897 by Clara Schlaffhorst and Hedwig Andersen. It became the basis on which these two founded their Rotenburger Breathing School, which still flourishes in Germany today. The book is regularly brought up to date and still appears in new editions.*

I studied breathing with several of the German schools, but I am most deeply indebted to Elsa Gindler. My own method developed during my many years of teaching in Berlin and, since 1940, in New York City. In both countries I found a real need for breathing work. It greatly benefited all my students, whether they needed their breath professionally as musicians, actors, or teachers, for heavy physical work, or simply for everyday life.

Nowadays breathing work is part of all physical reeducation programs abroad, and its importance to one's general well-being is fully recognized. Only recently has an interest developed in the United States in the role of breathing as an integral element of our bodily and emotional equilibrium. I hope this book will contribute to the growth of this interest and lead its readers to an understanding of how essential an adequate breathing support is and how caring for our breathing will enhance the quality of our lives.

* Leo Kofler, *The Art of Breathing as the Basis of Tone Production* (New York: Edgar S. Werner, 1889, 1890, 1893; 1st German ed., Cassel, Germany: Baerenreiter Verlag, 1897; 23d ed., 1966).

PART I
The Basics

1

The Role of Habits and the Best Way of Breathing

What causes poor breathing? What interferes with the quality of our breathing? Our way of life, of course. The stresses of modern times—war, crime, political unrest and upheaval, noise, air pollution, general and personal changes too sudden and too far-reaching for easy adjustment, mechanization threatening our sense of value as an individual—these are only a few of the difficulties that disturb our breathing.

Our breathing is affected by everything that happens to us—physical or emotional strain, injury, frustration, and even great success. Anything that goes on in us and around us has a simultaneous effect on our breathing. The free flow of air is hampered, exhalation is tampered with, and inhalation becomes insufficient. Breathing, a self-regulatory function, has the capacity to recover from strain and malfunctioning automatically as soon as the situation that caused the disturbance is over. Unfortunately, what usually happens is that instead of allowing our breathing to return and get back to normal in due time, we tend to interfere. Unconsciously and unintentionally, we often cling to the changed ways of breathing even after the events that brought on the disturbance have passed. At first this altered manner of breathing lasts for short periods, then for longer ones. Eventually it becomes habitual, and our breathing never regains its original undisturbed flow. For example, when you are startled by a sudden noise, you hold your breath, a perfectly normal reaction. The next time this happens, feel how long it takes you to let your breathing return to normal. Chances are you tend to hold onto the changed way of breathing well past the "emergency."

The experiments in this book will make you aware of how frequently a disturbed way of breathing is maintained after the initial disturbance has subsided. Most people are unaware that they do this. And, of course, only by becoming aware of poor habits can one try to overcome them.

Good breathing habits should be established early in life. Mothers and all those who care for infants should be alert to the processes of breathing recovery. Most people who pick up a baby in distress think they can lay the infant down as soon as he has stopped crying. But they should hold the baby closely, continuing to pat his back and comfort him, until he draws a deep breath. Only then has the infant's breathing normalized itself, and only then should you lay him down. This is a process so easy to observe that anyone alerted to it cannot possibly miss it. Good breathing habits, instead of poor ones, would thus be promoted.

To sum up: Our breathing reacts to any impact on us. We hold our breath when shocked, we restrain it under stress, and it is stimulated by joy. It is certainly not the aim of breathing work, nor is it possible, to have one's breathing unaffected by life or to avoid life's problems. On the contrary, contact with your breathing will make you more open to life's experiences. It will give you the resilience to cope with life's challenges and to enjoy its pleasures. You will learn to overcome the weariness that follows periods of poor breathing, to restore loss of energy, and you will experience full vitality as an unavoidable consequence of fuller breathing. You will be more aware of the vacillations in your breathing. You will learn how to induce changes in your breathing to overcome strain.

Acquiring this skill, though, can be a long process. It is not easy to overcome or change ingrained habits. We can rarely change habits from one moment to the next; most often we overcome them only gradually. Therefore you need to give yourself enough time. But since breathing work is so gratifying in all its phases, you will not mind the time involved nor the patience and perseverance needed.

Because of the diversity of influences on our breathing, it is obvious that there cannot be one best way of breathing. I emphasize this because as soon as people become aware of the inadequacy of their breathing habits, they invariably ask, "Now, what is the best way of breathing?" or "How should I breathe?" There is no *one* way of breathing that is *the* right way or *the* best way to be aimed for at all times. We breathe in many ways, and many ways of breathing may be appropriate. Breathing is right not when it functions all the time in one particular "ideal" manner, but when it works in a way that lets it freely adjust, changing its quality according to our needs of the moment, so that it will adequately support us as we face the diverse challenges of our lives. Running requires a different kind of breathing from sleeping, alertness for an important interview a different quality of breathing from that for a casual chat with a friend. Anger will make us breathe differently from serenity. A certain kind of breathing may be right for one situation but inadequate for another. Sometimes a very full breath will be appropriate; other times a much shallower one. There is just no one best way of breathing.

2

Method of Working

If you riffled through the pages of this book before you started to read it, you may have wondered what "breathing experiments" could be. Most physical education systems use exercises to achieve their aims. These involve executing predetermined, fixed sequences of activities. Improvement is expected to be gained by repetition. The more you repeat the exercises, the better, supposedly, the result.

Such a mechanistic approach is futile as far as breathing is concerned. Changes in the quality of breathing have to be achieved in a totally different way, through experimentation.

Breathing varies continuously, automatically and perfectly adjusting to our activities, provided we do not interfere. Though we often do interfere with these adjustments, we cannot inhibit these changes altogether. Breathing remains an involuntary, self-regulatory function. It changes not only with physical activity but also with every emotional impact; both pleasure and pain are mirrored in our breathing.

Breathing being so variable, it would be impossible to invent the multitude of exercises necessary for the innumerable shadings in the quality of our breathing. And, of course, one could not begin to remember and repeat them!

Further, breathing is basically a self-regulatory function. You cannot possibly exercise something that is self-regulatory. Only willful actions can be repeated or "exercised."

We cannot "make" breathing as we can "make" a movement. Breathing can only be provoked, coaxed, induced to change on its own. This can be done by certain beneficial stimuli. After providing a stimulus, we must try to let the reactions to it develop as freely as possible. These reactions will be involuntary. They happen *to* us: we cannot make them; we can only try to let them through. This way of working with breathing is what is called "experimenting."

The experiments described in Part II of this book are a series of proved stimuli to breathing. I say "proved" so that the word *experimenting* will not convey the idea that what is going to happen when you do an experiment is totally unknown. In a general way, the reactions to a specific stimulus can be foreseen. However, the actual course of the processes that ensue, the sequence in which changes take place, and the time involved will vary greatly. Reactions will depend on the momentary physical condition of the individual, on his or her mood, as well as on his or her experience of becoming aware of processes related to breathing and of letting changes in breathing through. You will understand that in spite of acquired experience and skill, you will not react as quickly or as easily to a stimulus when you are tired as when you are rested, when you have a headache as when you don't, when you are upset as when you are happy. These are only a few of the variables involved. And certainly do not underestimate the resistance against any kind of change that most of us have, which also greatly influences the processes.

Most beginners need a good deal of time to become aware of their reactions to a stimulus and to let these reactions develop freely. At first, responses may develop only partially and slowly. However, once you have done the experiments more often, you will recognize one of the most rewarding features of breathing work, which is to experience how quickly reactions to a stimulus can set in and how thoroughly far-reaching the changes in the quality of your breathing become in a surprisingly short period of time. A student who planned breathing work during her summer vacation gave the following report: "Oh, well, I really didn't have to do anything. Whenever I felt my breathing, I just let it recover, and my breathing was fine!" But to be able to let one's breathing recuperate and change that easily and that fast is the result of long work and experience.

When doing experiments, you need feedback. In breathing work, you rely on your body sense (kinesthetic sense), which enables you to become aware of yourself—not only to feel the position of your body in space but also to become aware of its condition. The sensations delivered inform you of the state of your breathing and of your reactions to the experiments. Like any of your senses, it can be highly developed and then used with greater efficiency. The more you use your body sense, the more developed it will become. Just as the trained musician hears details in a piece of music that the ordinary listener does not, you will find yourself sensing ever more about your breathing as soon as you begin consciously to use your body sense.

Unfortunately, intellectual development, not the development of our body sense, is emphasized in our culture. The body sense is usually applied in reference to pain. A new student proved this to me when answering my question as to what she could feel of her breathing, by saying, "Nothing aches." As if we should be aware only of discomfort! Thus many people are deprived of enjoying their own well-being. And they do not become aware early enough when something does begin to go wrong, and thus miss an opportunity to prevent serious trouble.

Movement is one way of activating our body sense. But we move less than prior generations did. Machines have taken over so much of the work for which bodily action was formerly needed, depriving us of many opportunities to develop our body sense. Sports, if done at all, usually involve the body in too specialized a way to give the variety of movement needed. And all too often sports training is so mechanical that it does not develop any sensing of the body at all.

Feeling yourself when experimenting does not mean that all you have previously learned about breathing is useless. Any scientific knowledge will be helpful in understanding your reactions to the experiments. Your first sensations when you begin to feel your breathing may be hazy and diffused. This should not be surprising, as most people are not in the habit of sensing their breathing at all. As you progress, however, you will become aware with great clarity of innumerable variations in the quality of your breathing and of exactly how your breathing reacts to specific experiments. Eventually it will be easy for you to become aware of your breathing.

At first, the end results of your work will be the easiest to feel. You will sense that your breathing is different from when you began the experiment. Later on, breathing sensations will become clear and irrepressible. As you become more skilled, you will be able to feel breathing changes as they are occurring. This is important. It is much easier to give in to these changes the moment you feel they are trying to break through. The more adept you become at feeling your breathing and allowing it to change, the faster and more far-reaching the impact of the experiments will be. This will shorten the time of your recovery from poor breathing states in your daily life. Not only will it make your everyday hustle less strenuous, but it will also enable you to enjoy all pleasant moments to the hilt.

3

Sensations Related to Breathing

The sensations experienced when doing the experiments are often misinterpreted. They are never sensations of breathing itself. They are only *sensations related to breathing*. In their healthy state, neither diaphragm, lungs, nor the exchange of gases can actually be felt. What we do sense are the effects of breathing, influences of the breathing process on the body, changes that take place in relation to breathing. When people say "I feel my lungs filling with air," they are not really feeling their lungs. What they feel is a widening of the chest cage as it accommodates the incoming air. This is a sensation related to the filling of the lungs, but not the feeling of the lungs themselves. Such feelings and impressions initiated by the breathing process are the tools used in breathing work.

Sensations related to breathing can be felt in areas close to the lungs, such as the nose, mouth, chest, and abdomen, or farther away, in the arms or legs. The sensations in the extremities are mainly of circulatory influences derived from changes in breathing. In addition, you cannot miss feeling changes in your emotional states during your breathing work and afterward.

To explain this further, here are a few examples of sensations you may become aware of that are related to your breathing. First, you may feel the flow of air through your nose or mouth—just a little puff or a large amount of air. Breathing may be fast and shallow or slow and deep. You may feel irregularities in rhythm. You may experience sensations of frustration or satisfaction, as, for instance, the feeling of relief when an inhalation finally gets through (or "over the hump," as my students call it). Or you may become aware of a sensation of depth in breathing ("It is streaming as if out of a deep well," a student once commented).

As these few examples demonstrate, the sensations related to one's breathing are of an infinite variety. Because you cannot foretell what sensations may occur, breathing work is endlessly interesting. Every time you do an experiment, your awareness will increase, and often you will experience new sensations or variations on familiar ones. I hear comments and expressions of amazement about this all the time. Surely, like my students, you, too, will respond to the experiments with ever-renewed surprise: "I have never felt *that* before" or "I have felt it before, but *never quite like this.*"

4

The Breathing Pause

Everyone knows that we breathe rhythmically. Most people assume that our breathing functions in a two-part rhythm: exhalation—inhalation. This is not so. At some point during your breathing work, you will discover that the breathing rhythm has three components: exhalation—pause—inhalation. The pause fulfills a double purpose: a resting from the effort of the inhalation and a rallying of the energy needed for the next inhalation. The pause, therefore, is not an idle period when nothing is happening; it is a vital phase in the breathing process.

The duration of the pause is significant. If we interfere with the length of the breathing pause, shortening it even slightly, we find ourselves feeling "rushed" and "pressured," that well-known state that interferes so often with our sense of well-being and is such a generally acknowledged burden in our daily lives. We have all experienced how strained this kind of breathing leaves us. We pay dearly for it in inefficiency, weariness, and irritability.

When starting breathing work, you may not immediately have any feel for the pause in your breathing. You may not be able to sense it for quite a while, neither in the checkups (described in Chapter 10) nor during the experiments. But one day you will become aware of it, probably quite suddenly. It may confuse you or make you uncomfortable when suddenly you sense a delay before an inhalation sets in. But if you are anticipating such an occurrence, it will lose most of its confusing or irritating quality. Once this first confusion has passed, you will feel tremendously relieved whenever experiencing the pause in your breathing rhythm.

Once the three-part rhythm of your breathing has reestablished itself, you will cherish it very much. A full-length pause in your breathing rhythm gives great relief, eradicates the feeling of being under pressure, and has a calming effect not only on your breathing but on your whole person, physically as well as emotionally.

But do not try to "do" or "make" the pause willfully. Because breathing is an involuntary process, you could never intentionally make the pause right. Its duration varies as your breathing changes, adjusting itself to the manifold tasks confronting you. The rhythm of your breathing, of which the pause is a phase, has to reestablish itself on its own. It is a part of the continuous, though varying, rhythm of your breathing.

5

Speed of Recovery of Breathing

To anyone who works alone with this book, the speed with which he or she can achieve an improvement in breathing is important. The time varies greatly from individual to individual. The change can occur very quickly or very slowly. There are no rules, but certain factors do play a role in the time element.

Obviously, an inexperienced person will need more time to let breathing recover than will someone with experience. Occasionally, however, even when trying an experiment for the first time, a beginner can achieve a remarkably different, more satisfying way of breathing rather quickly.

Weather conditions also influence progress. Moderate temperatures and low humidity are favorable for breathing work and are time-cutting factors. On hot, humid days, it takes considerably longer to get your breathing up to par. Air pollution inevitably restricts breathing and prolongs the recovery period. The higher the pollution level and the longer it lasts, the more confined your breathing becomes. Then much more time is needed to recover from the shallow breathing and to eliminate dust and other pollutants so that deeper breathing can set in again. Do not try to breathe deeply outside in a heavy smog. But do make up for the shallow breaths taken outdoors when you are inside again.

The speed with which your breathing can recover is also greatly influenced by your emotional condition. If you are upset, unhappy, anxious—even overjoyed—you will need considerably more time for your breathing to recover than when you are in a placid mood.

The greatest obstacle to a quick breathing recovery is illness. It need not even be a serious illness. If you are just not feeling well, have a headache, or are getting a cold, you will find that your reactions to an experiment will be considerably delayed. At such times, be patient but persistent. Eventually you will succeed. I want to emphasize again that no one can foresee exactly what the sequence of reactions in breathing work will be, that there are no fixed rules—once in a while you may experience the opposite. You should always be prepared for the unexpected. For example, even when you are not well, change may come rapidly, as if your breathing had waited for the chance to be freed!

To sum up: Any day you start an experiment, you should allow whatever time it may take to let your breathing change. Because you reacted fast one day does not necessarily mean that you will react as quickly the next. Be flexible, let nature work at its own speed, and you will recuperate in the fastest way possible for you.

6

A Decisive Moment

In the course of your breathing work, when you have accomplished far-reaching changes, you will be faced with a baffling experience. Finally able to feel and recognize certain typical sensations of your breathing, suddenly, during an experiment, you may become aware that all of these sensations have disappeared. This disappearance may even create the impression of not breathing at all. As a consequence, you may experience something close to anxiety.

But soon thereafter you will realize that only your manner of breathing has changed. And for the better! Instead of feeling sensations of laboring, irregularity, and difficulty in letting deeper breaths through—or whatever your usual sensations were—suddenly you cannot feel anything of the kind. All your old landmarks have vanished, and you experience a seeming vacuum.

When they reach this state, my students invariably comment with a puzzled, slightly anxious voice, "I don't seem to be breathing at all." Of course they are, and so are you. When this feeling occurs, you have left your old ways of breathing behind—at least for a while. At this moment,

16

familiar sensations are lost. They were mainly sensations of the difficulties that your habitual ways of breathing presented and of the emergency measures these conditions produced. Now that the quality of your breathing has changed, you will, after the period of puzzlement has passed, become aware of new characteristics and acquire new and different landmarks.

Therefore keep calm when this moment occurs. Try to feel your breathing anew. Become acquainted with the sensations of a less disturbed, more involuntary, quite different quality of breathing. "Breathing is so unobtrusive, so gentle, and so full at the same time"—that is how my amazed students often describe this state of their breathing.

The most impressive and most surprising sensation, though, is how extremely quietly and effortlessly breathing flows and how still you have to be to perceive these new sensations. All this means that you have achieved a striking difference in the quality of your breathing. Enjoy it!

Try as quickly as possible to recognize this fleeting moment of insecurity when it happens so that you will not be too baffled or anxious to continue. It is one of the important thresholds in your breathing work, a really decisive moment.

7

Emergency Measures

Since breathing is a vital function of the body, the body is equipped with various measures to sustain it in emergencies. These emergency measures do not become activated only in life-or-death situations; they are part of your daily life. For instance, they are involved in the process of awakening as well as in coming to the rescue when you are tired. You will encounter emergency measures during various stages of your breathing work.

Some of your initial reactions to breathing work may surprise you. Instead of getting the desired, easy, and full breathing you rightfully expected, you may discover that you have provoked only a breathing turmoil. Whenever your breathing is stimulated to function fully or to quiet down from overexcitation, emergency measures come into play to support the process. Recognition of these processes is important for your breathing work, particularly if you venture out on your own, with only this book for guidance.

You should not mistake emergency measures for good breathing. Recognize them for what they are: involuntary, helpful, temporary measures.

Understand what their purpose is and what their eventual disappearance means. Then, instead of being confused or irritated, you will be better able to judge the extent of a breathing disturbance and of any progress in recuperation. *Easy accommodation of emergency measures shortens their duration.*

In fact, at first you will have more experience with emergency measures than with good breathing. Ordinarily, poor breathing habits curtail our breathing to the extent that it serves only for mere survival. The need for a fuller exchange of gases may be so great that any stimulus produced through breathing experiments is bound at first to provoke emergency measures to achieve recovery as thoroughly and speedily as possible.

Emergency measures come into play not only in the beginning phases of your work, but also later on, whenever you need to recover from a period of poor breathing. Becoming aware of traces of emergency processes during the day will help to alert you to take care of your breathing.

Emergency measures fade out gradually during the course of a work session as the need for them subsides. You will then find yourself in a state of comfortable, easy breathing, ready to enjoy the true breathing work that can begin only after this emergency phase of your breathing has been overcome.

The emergency measures you will encounter most often during breathing work are yawning, rising shoulders, sighing or "heaving," stretching, and widening nostrils.

I. YAWNING

Yawning will probably be the first emergency measure brought into play through a breathing experiment. The lucky ones among us will immediately draw deeper breaths, but most of us will respond with the urge to yawn once or twice. Occasionally you may have to accept a spell of yawning. These yawns are not a sign of tiredness or boredom, though we do yawn when experiencing those conditions. When tired, we are in need of a resupply of oxygen; when we are bored, our breathing becomes shallower and shallower until the point when the emergency measure, yawning, has to set in to bring us back to normal breathing efficiency. (This last state of emergency is well characterized by the phrase "bored to death.")

Yawning is provoked by a violent contraction of the diaphragm, resulting in a massive exchange of air. Both exhalation and inhalation are extraordinarily increased. You will have to yawn until the equilibrium between oxygen and carbon dioxide in the body has reestablished itself. Then yawning subsides, and satisfying breaths can stream in with ease. Be prepared, though, when you continue the experiment, for the intensity of your breathing to increase and possibly induce another series of yawns. Welcome the emergency phase of yawning and try not to impede its course. The social law against yawning in public may create difficulties for some. In most social situations we are expected to be alert and attentive. Unfortunately, this "anti-yawn law" has been so strictly enforced that people sometimes have trouble yawning even when alone.

You need energy to yawn. If you happen to be tired, you may not be able to yawn immediately after a stimulus to your breathing. It may take a few tries until a full, strong yawn can be achieved ("to get a yawn through," as my students put it). Your diaphragm can only gradually recover the tonus necessary for the vigorous action that produces yawning.

It may sound odd, but there is intelligence involved in yawning successfully. Let your mouth open wide. Do not fight a yawn, but accommodate it and let the yawn subside on its own. Do not "bite it off" by closing your mouth prematurely. Try to keep your neck long, your head high and well balanced. Do not let your head tilt backward during yawning. When the yawn is over, feel whether your breathing has changed in quality, whether its performance is now different from before. Let this difference settle in by waiting out a couple of breaths before you repeat your experiment.

II. RISING SHOULDERS

An important and effective emergency measure occurs when your shoulders and collarbone rise involuntarily to facilitate inhalations. This is so helpful that it comes into play with almost all the other emergency measures. You will become aware when starting breathing experiments that whenever you succeed in letting a fuller breath through, your shoulders —that is, your shoulder blades and collarbones—rise involuntarily at the same time, taking your arms along in the action. Having the weight of all these parts lifted from your chest cage of course makes it considerably easier for the ribs underneath to expand. This emergency measure, regardless of what may be the cause of the breathing insufficiency, will be activated as long as there is still a struggle to let air flow in. Once an adequate elasticity of the rib cage and stronger action of the diaphragm have been reestablished, there will be no further need for such a drastic aid to inhalations. One mark of good breathing, as you will experience in time, is that your breaths will flow in without a struggle, without your having to lift weight off your chest cage to accommodate them.

III. SIGHING

Sighing is one of the emergency measures usually combined with rising shoulders. Sighing, or "heaving," as my students call this kind of breath, is an audible inhalation, considerably longer than the preceding ones. It is followed by a fast, also slightly audible exhalation. Sighing is a sudden break from a period of extremely shallow breathing. Though generally associated with recuperation from shock or grief, it is also brought on by habitually poor breathing. A large number of people, poor breathers all, seem to survive by sighing from time to time to bring their breathing up to a minimum standard, a habit that, understandably, greatly annoys those around them. However, when you feel an urge to sigh during breathing work, enjoy the relief it will give you and accept it as an emergency measure. Try to avoid returning to the poor way of breathing that preceded the sighing. Let it be the decisive breath after which an easier, more expansive way of breathing can stay with you.

IV. STRETCHING

Stretching is another highly efficient emergency measure. This is the same kind of stretch that you know well as a part of your awakening from sleep. The urge to stretch originates in the trunk and penetrates into the arm, often a bent arm; the elbow bends as a lead into the stretch, which then elongates the arm to its full length and extends to the fists or fingertips. The urge may also involve your legs.

After having worked for a while with a breathing experiment, you will feel an urge to stretch. Whenever you feel like stretching, immediately interrupt your work to do so. Stretch to your heart's delight—upward, sideways, diagonally, or downward. In short, stretch in any direction away from the center of your body. Stretch gently and carefully. Feel how far—sometimes only very little—you are able to extend with your stretch. It should always feel good, be a relief, and never be forced. If you were overtense or flabby at the beginning, you will find that your muscle tone changes as soon as your breathing recuperates. Your body is then eager to regain, through stretching, the length and width that were curtailed. Your lungs, being more active, also need more space. Consequently the urge to stretch breaks through.

Stretching is perhaps the most pleasant of all emergency measures. Let it happen as freely as you can. Whether you stretch one arm or both arms, one leg or both legs, whether you feel like wiggling your back or neck to gain length, give in and stretch. Ease out from your stretch slowly and gently. Feel how much of the elongation you achieved through the stretch stays with you. Try to avoid stiffening up afterward or collapsing back into your former state. Feel how much basic change your stretching brought about. When you do a checkup (see Chapter 10) after stretching successfully, you will feel that your breathing is working more easily, more fully, more satisfactorily than before. Stretching has relieved the squeezing, the foreshortening of your joints, and the pressure on your rib cage. Your whole body is now fit for action, more invigorated, with more energy available for breathing.

V. WIDENING NOSTRILS

Widening the nostrils is the least efficient emergency measure. It may happen with inhalations when a fuller than habitual breath struggles through. But this involuntary pulling apart of your nostrils has no real effect on inhalation. I believe this to have been a trait of prehistoric people that by now has lost its usefulness.

8

Stumbling Blocks

Before beginning the breathing experiments, I would like to alert you to certain phases that will occur in your work that might puzzle you. Hyperventilation (overbreathing), pains in the back, discharge from nose and throat, belching, and hunger sensations are the major stumbling blocks you will encounter in the course of your breathing work. They are temporary occurrences and easily taken care of. Though seeming to be obstacles, these stumbling blocks are, in fact, proof of success. You need to be able to recognize them and know how to help yourself so that neither suffering nor misunderstanding keeps you from continuing your breathing experiments.

I. HYPERVENTILATION

Everyone, sooner or later, after having responded well to a breathing experiment and having achieved a fuller than habitual way of breathing, will hyperventilate occasionally. Hyperventilation is the state that results from having breathed so deeply that you have more oxygen in your blood than you can handle just yet. In time, your tolerance for oxygen will increase as your vital capacity (your standard of breathing) increases through breathing work.

You can recognize hyperventilation by a slight *dizziness* (feeling "a bit funny in the head," my students call it). Hyperventilation may develop slowly or may overcome you rather suddenly, sometimes between one breath and the next. The remedy is simple: Use up the not-yet-tolerable oxygen. A few vigorous movements will do that. Jump up and down on both feet a couple of times, walk around briskly, or thrust your arms out several times energetically with your fists clenched and hold your arms for a moment in the thrust position (Figure 2). Actually, any somewhat vigorous movement will do.

As soon as your head feels clear again, continue with your experiment. Should you, however, become dizzy again almost immediately when you proceed, stop working for the time being. You may need to wait for an hour or more or even until the next day before continuing. Hyperventilation particularly troubles beginners. It may be precipitated by the aftereffects of an illness or by your having been a poor breather for a long time. You should then do breathing work for short periods only.

As soon as your average way of breathing becomes more efficient, you will rarely hyperventilate. Your body will be accustomed to deeper breathing and hence will tolerate more oxygen. You will discover that you can do breathing work for longer and longer periods without hyperventilating.

Another sign of hyperventilation is a feeling of overwhelming *tiredness*; this can also arise quite suddenly, or it may come on gradually. As soon as you feel it, interrupt your work and do some vigorous movements like those mentioned above to use up the overabundance of oxygen. Continue only when you feel alert again.

Sometimes a feeling of slight *malaise* may be the only way in which hyperventilation shows itself. You just do not feel right. Since you ordinarily feel better when your breathing improves, this feeling of a sort of general discomfort is a sure sign of hyperventilation. Again, interrupt immediately. Move briskly in any way you like to use up the oxygen you cannot yet tolerate. Continue only when comfortable again.

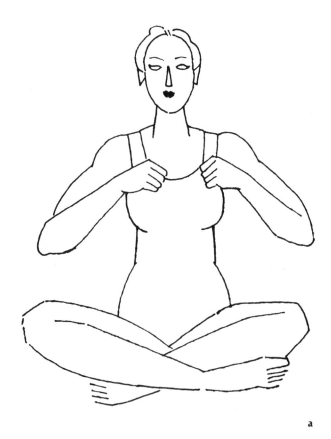

a

Figure 2. Overcoming hyperventilation.

b

Figure 3. Areas in the back where temporary discomfort may occur.

II. BACK PAINS

Beginners may frequently be bothered by slight backaches during an experiment. Though this may sound contradictory, such a predicament is a sign of success.

Only if your breathing has become considerably more lively is there a need for a fuller expansion of your chest cage. If your muscles are not elastic enough to yield the necessary widening—and they probably are not —a strong tug is applied on them. This tug causes your discomfort. As soon as this "tug-of-war" between your breath wanting to expand the chest cage and the stiff musculature resisting it is over, you will no longer get back pains. Although back pains may occur anywhere, the areas most often affected are the horizontal rectangle below the shoulder blades, the area between the shoulder blades, and the small of the back (Figure 3).

Like hyperventilation, pains in the back are particularly a beginner's dilemma, though such pains may recur during any phase of your breathing work. These back pains are easily relieved. Interrupt your work and tap yourself briskly* wherever you are uncomfortable. Tap firmly with the palm of your hand or the side of your fist, or use a Japanese back tapper.†

A couple of relatively brisk—but never rough—taps are usually enough to relieve such momentary discomfort. The muscles are loosened up through the vibration of the tapping and then can yield to accommodate the needed expansion of your chest cage. Do not be heroic and try to wait out the discomfort. Tap as soon as you feel that an ache might develop. Again, during the beginning phase of your breathing work, you may have to interrupt and tap yourself fairly often. Later on, you will rarely have to tap your back.

III. DISCHARGE FROM NOSE AND THROAT

If your nose, sinuses, or bronchi are not in good condition, affected by air pollution, allergies, or colds, you will find that when doing breathing

---

* This way of tapping briskly to ease backache is not the kind of tapping applied to stimulate your breathing as described in Part II, Chapter 12.
† These tappers are available in Japanese novelty stores.

experiments you will have to blow your nose or cough up phlegm, sometimes profusely. Therefore, keep tissues or a handkerchief handy.

The stimulation of your breathing brings about a contraction of the mucous membranes in your nose, throat, and bronchi. Your body is then able to discharge what was blocked in these passages, and your breathing becomes much easier and fuller. Well-functioning passageways are needed for the flow of air during exhalations and inhalations. Your breathing work will contribute greatly to clearing these areas for a freer flow of air.

IV. BELCHING AND HUNGER SENSATIONS

When your breathing becomes fuller, the downward excursion of your diaphragm increases. The stomach, which is situated directly beneath the diaphragm, will then be pressed upon in a much stronger, rather unaccustomed manner. It may react to this sudden compression by contracting, thus expelling air through belching, or giving off the sensation of hunger, even when, in fact, you could not be hungry at that time. The periods of belching as well as those of hunger pangs are of short duration and sure signs that your breathing has become more powerful.

9

Technicalities

Before presenting the experiments, I would like to comment on technicalities concerning breathing work and answer, in advance, questions that may come up when you want to begin the work. I hope that this will eliminate the uncertainties that frequently haunt beginners, and thus will get you off to a good start.

Time of Day for Work

No particular time of day is *the* best time for everybody. Choose whatever time fits most conveniently into your particular life-style, making sure to choose the time when you are least likely to be disturbed. The only times that are unsuitable for breathing work are the two hours after a meal and the last moments before going to bed.

The early morning, just after getting out of bed, is when most people urgently need to attend to their breathing. Doing your experiments then helps to overcome morning sluggishness. If you did not sleep well or long enough, breathing work will banish your tiredness. In fact, it is worth rising earlier to have time for breathing work, as it will invariably set you up for the day's challenges.

Do not choose the time before going to bed as a work period because, being tired, you will have difficulty concentrating. And even if you succeed, you will then be wide-awake. Instead, use this time to apply all your experiences with breathing. Lying in bed in your favorite sleeping position, do a breathing experiment and let your reactions through without studying them; just enjoy the results. You will become calm, your anxieties will be soothed, your mind will be emptied of the day's excitements and troubles, and you will overcome that nervous exhaustion that tends to keep you from falling asleep. I call these moments "harvest time," moments when you do not "study" but make use of the skills you have acquired to get ready for a good, recuperative sleep.

Place for Breathing Work

You can do your breathing work anywhere. But for extended work sessions choose a quiet place where you will be undisturbed by noise or people. In good weather, open a window or work outside. Under any circumstances, avoid working where you are exposed to drafts.

Room Temperature

This, too, like the time of day you choose, is a matter of personal preference. Some people work better in a warmer room, others in a cooler one. Choose whatever temperature you prefer, but make sure not to get chilled. Being uncomfortably cool will slow down and hamper your responses and thus make it much harder for you to react to breathing experiments.

Clothing

No special clothing is needed. Wear something comfortable. Loosen a belt, brassiere, or collar that might prevent you from breathing freely. If it is warm enough, slip into a sleeveless leotard or loose-fitting bathing trunks. The less covered you are, the more your skin will be aired, and this airing is a helpful stimulus to breathing. However, be sure to keep yourself warm enough (even wrapping up in a blanket if necessary).

Position

The best position is sitting cross-legged on a mat, rug, or blanket, without shoes (they interfere with the circulation in your feet). (See Figure 4.) If you feel uncomfortable without back support, sit with your pelvis and back against a wall. Eventually your fuller breathing will buoy you up enough so that you will be able to sit freely without support, even for long periods. Muscles and joints that may not be accustomed to this position will adjust in time.

Another good position, easier for some people, is to kneel and then sit down on their feet (Figure 5).

Any discomfort in sitting will interfere with your work. So if you cannot sit comfortably for any length of time in either of the above-mentioned positions, sit on a chair, preferably one with a level seat and a straight back. Sit with your back unsupported, if you can do it without strain, or support your pelvis and back against the back of the chair. Should the seat of the chair not be level, even it with a pillow or sit on the edge. If the chair has a slanted back, turn it sideways to a wall and utilize the wall as support. The seat of the chair should be low enough so that your thighs are horizontal to the floor. Rest your feet on a footstool or book if necessary. Your ankles should be vertically underneath your knees, and the soles of your feet should rest on the floor (Figure 6).

Lying down is not recommended because you might easily become too relaxed and fall asleep. (If you are sick and in bed and your doctor has no objection to gentle breathing work, then of course you have to do your breathing work lying down. But make it a point to remain alert.)

These positions are by no means the only ones for breathing work, but they are preferable. After all, we breathe in whatever position we find ourselves, so virtually any position can be taken.

Length of Work Period

No particular time limit need be set for the length of a breathing work session. It can be five minutes, ten minutes, a half hour, or longer. A sure sign that you can continue is the feeling of well-being that you should always attain through the experiments. Therefore you can work for as long or as short a time as you feel comfortable. Hyperventilation or backache are reasons to interrupt, shorten, or end your period of work. (Then proceed as explained in Chapter 8.) Another reason to pause is the general feeling that you need a break after having done an experiment for some time.

Figure 4. Sitting crosslegged for breathing work, with supported back if necessary.

Figure 5. Kneeling and sitting on feet for breathing work.

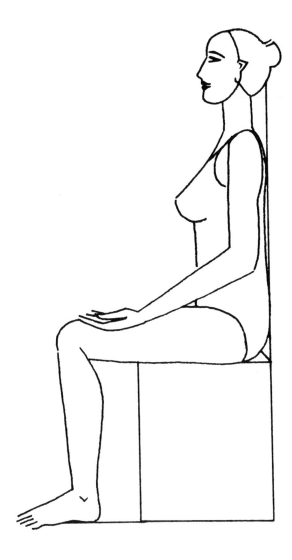

Figure 6. Sitting for breathing work on chair with supported back.

Then by all means stretch, lie down for a short rest, or walk around a bit. After such an interruption you should be able to continue. But never force yourself; breathing work is not an endurance test.

Lack of concentration will probably be more of an obstacle to longer work periods than bodily difficulties. You will find, though, that gradually you will be able to concentrate longer and longer on breathing experiments. This increase in your power of concentration is one of the particularly useful side effects of breathing work.

Order of the Experiments

The sequence in which the experiments are presented in this book has been carefully determined. When beginning your breathing work, follow this order closely. However, the first three experiments are interchangeable. Try each for a couple of days; then choose the one to which you reacted particularly well, and start your work with that one. Stay with it for quite a while before going on to another one. Once you have enough experience, you can use any experiment you feel a need for, regardless of its order in the book. Choose freely whichever one seems most appropriate to help your condition at the moment.

Do not try an experiment just once and then take up the next one. Work with each for *many* sessions. You can stay with one experiment for months if it serves your needs well. Of course, after a certain time, your responses to a particular stimulus become dulled—a perfectly normal reaction. At this point your concentration will begin to waver more than usual. The results of your work will not be as satisfactory as before, or you may feel that the breathing problem that made you choose this particular experiment has been solved. Then it is time to change to another experiment. This does not mean that the first experiment can never be helpful again. If you try it sometime later, you will find that you again react well to it.

To repeat: Stay with the same experiment for as long as you do not become dulled to it. Change to another when you find yourself no longer responding as well as could be expected. But do not flit like a butterfly from one to another. That will only rob you of the chance to achieve a worthwhile change in the quality of your breathing, and you will be left frustrated and disappointed.

PART II
The Experiments

10

The Checkup

The purpose of the checkup is to become aware of the state of your breathing. It will enable you to compare, evaluate, and appreciate the differences in the state of your breathing arrived at through an experiment. This evaluation is of vital importance for successful breathing work. Not only vague impressions but clearly felt sensations should be your guide.

Better breathing feels so right, in many ways so utterly normal, that without comparison you will often miss the decisive difference in the quality of your breathing that you may have achieved. The checkup is the only way to get an objective assessment of the various states of your breathing and of progress or failure in your work. *That is why it should be done before and after each session.*

A checkup can be done quickly, as only a general impression of your breathing is needed. Awareness of all details of your condition is not necessary. The checkup should take only a few moments before and after a session of breathing work. One more reason to make it a quick procedure, particularly for beginners, is the fact that your breathing changes as soon as you try to become aware of it. You may disturb it or let it change for the better almost instantaneously.

There are several questions to ask yourself that will make it easier to do a checkup.

First Question:

"Do I feel anything at all that is related to my breathing?" This question will soon change to: "What do I feel that is related to my breathing?"— because after a few attempts there will be no doubt that you are able to feel something related to your breathing.

The first few times, this may be a troublesome question, and no answer may be forthcoming. It may seem as if you are not feeling anything and cannot become aware of anything related to your breathing at all. But this is not so. New students often mention this at the beginning of a session. However, at the end of the work period, when they are making another checkup, they report all sorts of changes in their breathing. They feel their breathing "deeper," or "more in the abdomen," or "much stronger," or they comment, "I don't have to labor for breath so much anymore." These statements prove clearly that they must have had impressions of their breathing, without realizing it, when they did the checkup at the beginning. How else could they make such specific comparisons at the end of the session? They became able to feel sensations of their breathing consciously and therefore could recognize and verbalize the differences.

For most of us, sensitivity to breathing is an extremely undeveloped faculty, but one that will develop as you do the experiments in this book. Patience is needed, though. I stress this point about the elusiveness of most early impressions so that discouragement during the beginning work sessions can be avoided. *Continue to do the checkups even if at first you are disappointed and puzzled by the lack of clear sensations.*

Second Question:

"Where, specifically, do I feel something that is related to my breathing?"

Which areas of your body do you feel are involved in your breathing? To which areas does your breathing "spread"? Do you feel it only in your nose or neck, or in your upper chest and nowhere else? With your second checkup, at the end of your work session, you may feel many other areas involved in your breathing, such as your sides, abdomen, or back.

Third Question:

"*What does my breathing feel like?*"

What are its characteristics, its quality? Is it labored, easy, restricted, full, shallow, rhythmic, weak, jerky? These are some typical characteristics of breathing, examples of what you might experience when you do a checkup, not sensations you should look for or feel obliged to have.

Let me point out once more why the checkups are so essential. First of all, without the comparison through the checkups, you might not realize the changes in the quality of your breathing as the result of an experiment. Progress will be obvious, though, when you contrast the quality of your breathing at the beginning of a work period with that at the end of one. These changes will be enormously gratifying. Because you are working alone, with this book as your only guide, you will need all the encouragement and sure signs of progress available, which the checkups will give you.

And do not forget that the checkups should be done fast. Simply catch a few impressions quickly and leave it at that. Of course, you could discover more details about your breathing if you were to take more time. But you need only a general impression of your breathing to compare qualities.

Later on, when you are more experienced with breathing work, the checkup will take on an added dimension. Not only will it make you aware of the state of your breathing, but it will give you, in addition, the clue as to how to proceed—that is, what experiment to choose as the most appropriate to improve your condition.

Now that warnings and explanations have been given, you are ready to begin.

11

The Straw Experiment

Needed for this experiment: an ordinary drinking straw.

First do a checkup on your breathing. Keep in mind that because you are a beginner the checkup may upset your ordinary way of breathing. Therefore try as quickly as you can to get an impression of the state of your breathing. Even general, tentative impressions as to where and how you are breathing will enable you to make a comparison at the end of your session. Wait patiently and alertly until your breathing has quieted down and returned to a more ordinary way of functioning. Only then will you be ready to start the experiment.

For beginners, there is a double purpose in this experiment. First, it will give an opportunity to establish conscious contact with your breathing. Second, the experiment itself will help you to allow your exhalations to stream out more of their own accord. That may sound simple, but it is not.

Begin the experiment by feeling when your exhalations and inhalations occur. When you have become aware of that, and shortly after an average exhalation has begun, put the straw in your mouth and let the air pass

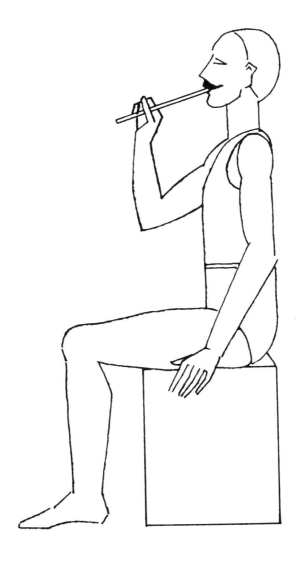

Figure 7. Straw Experiment.

through it instead of through your nose (Figure 7). Feel whether your exhalation passed through of its own accord, or whether you interfered. Try not to help at all; not to blow, push, or force. You will only gradually become aware of the extent of your interferences. Remove the straw just before the end of your exhalation, and let the rest of the air pass through your nose.

In case you are not sure whether all the air is passing through the straw, hold your nose during exhalations the first few times.

Raise the straw up to your mouth instead of bending down toward it. This will avoid strain or pressure on your neck and chest and will also prevent you from slumping.

All movements with the straw should be gentle and easy to prevent any disturbance of your breathing.

Allowing exhalations to begin before using the straw effectively blocks the tendency—strong among beginners—to get ready for the experiment by taking an extra-deep breath and then hoarding the air for exhalation through the straw. Such air can only get out explosively, just the opposite of what you are aiming for: a gentle, even flow of air.

Taking the straw out of your mouth shortly before the end of your exhalation and letting the rest of the air pass through your nose is a good way to avoid the temptation to press out that last bit of exhalation air instead of letting your exhalation end on its own.

In short: Avoid gulping air in and holding it before you start, and avoid forcing air out at the end of the exhalation.

After each exhalation through the straw, take time out to let all reactions to the experiment through. Allow your breathing to respond freely in any manner it may. Give in to yawning, heaving, sighing, stretching, or extra-deep breaths. Your whole body will respond. Your shoulders may drop, your back straighten out, and you may have many other reactions. Accommodate all changes as best you can. The exhalation through the straw is only the stimulus; *the reactions to the stimulus are what you are aiming for.*

Sometimes beginners find it difficult to feel anything special in response to the Straw Experiment. This is no reason to be discouraged. The speed with which you respond to the Straw Experiment depends not only on your goodwill but on your general condition as well. Being overtense (bodily cramped or emotionally overexcited) or flaccid (physically overtired or mentally and emotionally exhausted) will slow down your responses. And, most important, you need training to become aware of the ways in which your body reacts to a breathing experiment. Therefore the more experienced you become, the quicker and more far-reaching your responses will be and the easier it will become for you to sense changes in your breathing.

Reactions to the Straw Experiment are manifold. Some people are fortunate enough to be rewarded right away with satisfying, deep breaths. Others have to undergo the above-mentioned chain of reactions—yawning, gasping, stretching—before deeper breaths come through. Whenever they happen, enjoy them! You worked for them.

After a while you will feel that the phase of the strong reactions is over, that an average way of breathing has reestablished itself, and that each breath is more or less like the one before. You are now ready to repeat the experiment.

When beginning, unless hyperventilation forces you to interrupt even earlier, you may do this experiment for about five minutes. Extend your work periods gradually, up to a half hour or longer.

What will tempt you to work longer is the spectacular change in your breathing. Even at an early stage you will observe improvement. One of my students described his progress this way: "At first I always felt as though I were breathing through three blankets, and now—after ten minutes of work—it feels like only one blanket."

Breathing through the straw is effective for several reasons. By letting the air stream out as freely as possible through the straw, you actually expel more air than you would ordinarily. This is the key to increased inhalation. The more air goes out, the more air has to come in. The pressure of the atmospheric air and the pressure of the air in the lungs have to equalize.

Furthermore, since the air can get out only slowly through the narrow straw, the diaphragm (your main breathing muscle) is forced to relax slowly rather than suddenly. This keeps it from becoming flabby, a condition that is the opposite of what you are aiming for. Slow relaxation of your diaphragm improves muscle tone, not only of the diaphragm itself but also of

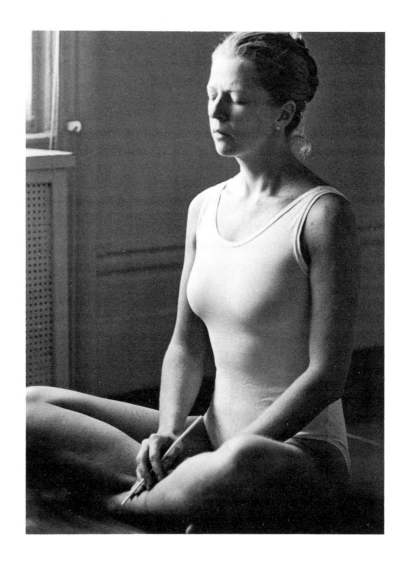

Figure 8. Straw Experiment: Taking time to let reactions through.

secondary breathing muscles (for example, your abdominal and trunk musculature as well as muscle tonus all through your body). As soon as your breathing apparatus is toned up right, more efficient breathing follows.

Finally, the more you succeed in eliminating your interference with exhalations, the less strained your breathing will be and the more effortlessly and satisfyingly your breath will flow.

Also, the Straw Experiment provides you with a simple and objective test to check the quality of your breathing. With the palm of your hand, feel the temperature of the first and last exhalation you let pass through the straw. You will discover that the air at the end of the work session is considerably warmer than your first exhalation through the straw was. As air coming from deeper parts of your body is warmer, this indicates that your breathing is deeper, less superficial than when you began.

12

The Tapping Experiments

Tapping is one of the ways by which you can influence the condition of the body. It is used in massage; a baby's back is tapped to calm him or her; and you yourself may tap someone's upper back to encourage or assure the person of your goodwill. You may also tap someone's bottom out of sheer joie de vivre. A hard tap makes muscles stiffen, while a gentle tap eases them. Every tap creates a vibration. Tapping your chest cage creates vibrations in the musculature of the chest cage that penetrate to the lungs, which, in turn, respond to the stimulus with fuller breathing.

To tap the chest cage, cup your hand slightly, as if you wanted to tap with air in your palm (Figure 9). Tap ever so gently with your cupped hand, three or four times in succession. Practice the light tap a few times on your leg or arm to get the feel for the movement until you achieve a light, pleasant touch. Later, when you tap your chest cage, try to determine how light a tap is enough to make your lungs respond. To use more effort is unnecessary and, in fact, would disturb your breathing.

Do not tap on one spot only; cover a whole area. The easiest way is to tap the left side of your chest cage with your right hand, and vice versa.

Figure 9. Hand position for tapping the chest cage.

Make sure you do not hold your breath while tapping—beginners tend to do this. Holding the breath is a disturbance of breathing and will defeat the purpose of the experiment.

After a series of light taps, pause and let through all reactions that may develop in your breathing and in your whole body.

Study the illustrations and tap your chest cage, area after area, according to the sequence of the numbers in the pictures.

I. TAPPING THE UPPER CHEST CAGE

Begin by tapping one side of the upper front of your chest cage (area 1 in Figure 10). This area is delineated by the collarbone (clavicle), shoulder joint, breastbone (sternum), and breast. *Never tap the breast itself.*

Stop after a few taps and try to accommodate all reactions that want to come through. If you get no response at all, you may have tapped too gently. Then tap the same area once more with a slightly firmer touch.

The first reactions you may feel when doing this experiment may not be breathing reactions but circulatory ones. You may feel a tingling sensation or one of warmth in the area you tapped. Both reactions indicate that blood vessels are responding to the tapping. The tingling occurs when some, but not all, of these vessels have opened up; a feeling of warmth proves that all the vessels have opened and considerably fuller circulation has penetrated the area. These reactions are only the prelude to a true breathing response. That will happen later, as you continue and repeat the tapping. As soon as you feel breathing changes, let them through as freely as you can.

In the beginning, it may take a while to achieve breathing responses. You may have to tap an area repeatedly to achieve a satisfactory change in the

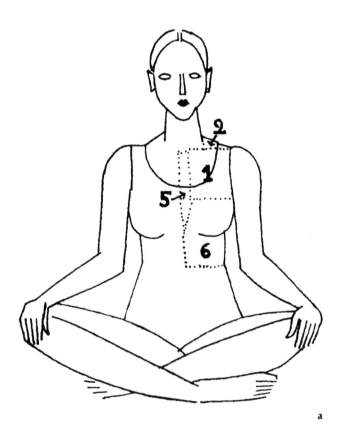

Figure 10. Areas for tapping, skinfold, and pressure experiments.

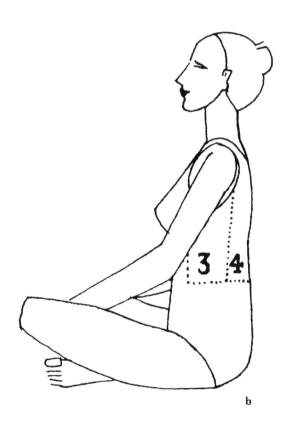

b

quality of your breathing. But as you continue to do this experiment, you will react much more quickly, eventually responding even to a single light tap.

When the reactions to a series of tappings subside in the area you have been tapping and you feel fairly satisfied with the changes in your breathing, you are ready to proceed to the next area.

II. TAPPING ABOVE THE COLLARBONE

Now tap over the triangle above the collarbone—that is, the area between the collarbone, the shoulder joint, the shoulder muscle (m. trapezius) and the neck (area 2 in Figure 10). *Never tap the neck.* (It contains sensitive glands that could be irritated by tapping.) If you have deep hollows just above the collarbone where the tips of your lungs are situated, you are making little use of those parts of your lungs. After you have done the breathing experiments for a while, these hollows will fill out, showing that the upper parts of your lungs are being used more fully.

After each series of tappings, try to let all your reactions through. By now you may begin experiencing true breathing responses. You may feel strong urges to yawn or to wriggle and stretch. You may draw one or more extremely deep and satisfying breaths. Give in to all reactions, whatever they may be. All changes in your breathing should be allowed to work themselves through.

As before, when you have tapped this area for a while and the phase of the strong reactions is over and your breathing is fairly calm again, you are ready to tap the next area of your chest cage.

III. TAPPING THE SIDE OF THE CHEST CAGE

This area includes your side from below the armpit to the bottom of your rib cage (area 3 in Figure 10). If in doubt about where your last rib is located, feel and trace it by hand before you begin tapping. Tap gently with your cupped hand all over your side. You may tap upward, downward, from back to front—however you prefer. As before, after a few taps, pause and let all your responses come through. Always permit your breathing to even out before you tap again.

IV. TAPPING THE BACK

Finally, tap as much of one-half of your back, from the shoulder down to the rim of your pelvis, as you can reach without strain (area 4 in Figure 10). You may be surprised to find that you can reach all of your back without difficulty. You can use one or both hands for tapping, simultaneously or one at a time. Reach with your hand from above as well as from below your shoulder, whichever way is easiest. If you are feeling a bit stiff or cannot quite reach everywhere, try tapping your back with a long-handled bath brush or a hairbrush. You may prefer the back of the brush for a slightly firmer tap, or you may want to use the bristles, which simultaneously provide stimulation to the skin. Be careful to tap gently, as the brush gives a harder tap than your hand. A Japanese back tapper is the most comfortable instrument for this purpose (see note p. 29).

Tapping the back is easiest, though, with the help of a partner. If someone else taps you, the problem of how to reach your whole back is solved. Demonstrate the tapping touch to your partner so that he or she understands and has felt how lightly it should be done. Definitely, no slapping; only tapping!

After completing the tapping of one-half of your chest cage, pause for a moment and compare the two halves of your trunk. What does the tapped half feel like? How does it compare with the other? What is your breathing like by now? You will be amazed at the extraordinary differences you are bound to feel between the tapped and untapped halves of your chest cage. Students describe the tapped areas of the trunk as "more there," "more alive," "larger"; or they say, "It feels as though only my tapped half is breathing."

At this point, a difficulty can arise. If you have tapped one-half of your chest cage for a prolonged time and its condition has changed considerably, this might cause the other half to ache. This is not serious and rarely happens. But if it should happen to you, stop and tap the aching side right away. When you even up the condition of the two halves of your chest cage, the discomfort will disappear.

Tapping stimulates not only breathing but circulation and muscle tone as well. Therefore it is a great help to getting going in the morning if you have a hard time starting the day. When arising, tap area after area of your chest cage either sitting or standing. At first it may take a while—perhaps as much as fifteen minutes—to feel alert and ready to do things. With more experience you will react much faster—in five minutes or less. But *never tap the chest cage before going to bed*, as it will make you too wide-awake for sleep.

When you begin these experiments, you may not be conscious of success immediately. A class member once reported no success with the early-morning tapping. She was the exception, as all the others reported becoming wide-awake, even when they were short of sleep. I urged the unresponsive student to keep trying for another week. She returned to class reporting that she still had not felt any response, but that something strange had happened to her. One morning she had forgotten to tap herself and, to her surprise, felt very uncomfortable all morning, as if she had forgotten to brush her teeth. She could hardly wait until lunch to do her tapping.

I mention this episode because at first you may have a similar problem in feeling changes in your breathing. In that case, interrupt your breathing work for a day or two and see if you feel a difference. This is a helpful way of checking your breathing work as long as your body awareness is not yet well developed.

Do not tap wherever you feel at all tender to tapping—whether it is in a small spot or a larger area. Try tapping there sometime later during the same work period or when you work the next time.

Tapping the chest cage can also come in very handy during the day whenever you feel yourself getting low on energy. It is a real pick-me-up. Even a short series of tappings will stimulate your breathing immediately and replenish your energy considerably.

Should tapping cause you to cough, postpone this experiment and choose another one. The cough may be the last trace of a cold. But if coughing persists whenever you tap, you should see your doctor.

Tapping, by the way, can be done not only as a complete experiment but, done briefly, also as a starter before other experiments to stimulate your breathing if you feel sluggish. For the same reason, it can also be inserted for short periods during other experiments.

V. TAPPING THE BREASTBONE BRISKLY

This tapping experiment should be done only considerably later than the others, when you have acquired ample experience with breathing. I mention it here only because it is also an experiment that uses tapping.

When the upper chest is sunken in and one's breathing feels weak, then tapping briskly over the breastbone (area 5 in Figure 10) gives great relief and restores breathing efficiency.

But the manner of tapping is different from the one applied to the chest cage in the previous experiments. When tapping your breastbone, cup your hand into a claw position (Figure 11). Use all your fingertips, except your thumb, simultaneously, or use only the tips of the index and third fingers of both hands, changing hands for each tap. Tap down and up on your breastbone. Tap fast, one hand following closely after the other. The fingertips should tap briskly on the breastbone, like little hammers. Do not tap the very end of the breastbone to avoid touching the stomach. All taps should be vigorous and firm.

Doing this once or twice down and up your breastbone is enough. Pause and give yourself time to let this strong stimulus affect you. Repeat the experiment as often as necessary, but only after all your reactions to each series of tappings have come through and your breathing has become even again.

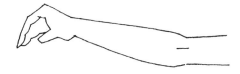

Figure 11. Claw position of hand for special tapping of breastbone.

Not many such tappings are needed to achieve a change in breathing quality and give you a quick reprieve from sluggishness. This experiment, so helpful for fast recuperation, can be slipped in during leisure time as well as at work. It will come in very handy in the brief times between interviews, before committee meetings, or whenever there is a need for breathing improvement and you have just a few moments at your disposal to initiate recuperation and restore energy.

13

The Open Mouth Experiment

In contrast to the Straw Experiment, which provides a narrow passageway for air, this experiment uses the largest possible passage—your wide open mouth.

After a checkup on your breathing, feel when your exhalations and inhalations occur. Shortly after the start of an ordinary exhalation, open your mouth wide and let the air stream out as freely as you can (Figure 12). The air should flow out of its own accord without even the slightest pushing or forcing on your part.

Aim for an easy, wide opening of your mouth; do not force it. You may discover that your jaw is—as happens frequently—quite cramped and does not lend itself to a wide opening. This will gradually improve as you repeat the experiment and try to let yourself ease up. Also, try to let your tongue rest on the bottom of your mouth and keep your throat and neck comfortably wide. This will be helpful in achieving an easy, wider opening of the mouth. Eventually with this experiment you will succeed in creating a passageway for exhalation that feels as wide as a barn door.

After a single exhalation through your open mouth, go back to breathing

Figure 12. Open Mouth Experiment.

through your nose again. Take time to let your breathing respond to the stimulus of the easy exit for the air. Let yourself yawn freely, heave, or gulp in air—whatever you have the urge to do. Try to feel what happens when you let the air stream out. Are you, in spite of your good intentions, still "helping" the air out? What does your breathing feel like when eventually you are able to force it less? What are the main characteristics of your breathing now?

When your breathing has evened out and you sense that there will be no more strong reactions, you are ready to try another exhalation through your open mouth.

In all experiments you should wait until an average way of breathing has reestablished itself. There are two reasons for this. Be economical with your efforts. Why do more work than necessary? If you re-stimulate your breathing while still reacting to a previous stimulus, your breathing will become erratic ("huddled up," as my students say); instead of getting more comfortable, you will be extremely uncomfortable for a while. To avoid this, take all the time you may need—and you may need quite a while—until your breathing becomes calm again before starting another experiment.

Though this is basically a simple experiment and easy to do, some people have difficulty with it. They are self-conscious and afraid of looking stupid with their mouths wide open. As long as you do not thrust your chin forward and let your head sink back flabbily as you open your mouth—which, of course, you should not do—you will look fine.

Whenever you stop working, feel your breathing. What is it like now? How does it compare with the way it felt when you started? You need to make frequent comparisons to become ever more familiar with the variations in your breathing quality and the ways in which your breathing can change.

The Straw, Tapping, and Open Mouth experiments are those best suited for beginners. Try each for a while. Their order is interchangeable. Start prolonged work first with the one that tempts you most and to which you react most easily and quickly.

14

The Sibilant "S" Experiment

The sibilant "S" is a hissing sound produced by letting an exhalation out through your mouth as you curl the sides of your tongue upward to touch your teeth, thus forming a channel for the air to pass through. This passing of air through a small channel produces the hissing sound. Aim for a long, loud, steady sound and project it horizontally forward. In contrast to the Straw and Open Mouth experiments, a certain effort is required to make a sibilant "S." The "S," however, should not start explosively. Do not press or force your breath out; let it flow freely. Forcing the "S" out will create pressure in your neck and head, which is certainly not desirable. Projecting the air out horizontally, straight forward not downward, will help to prevent your chest from slumping. The breathing of most beginners is so weak that they tend to let their upper chests collapse when exhaling with a sibilant "S."

This experiment offers one more way to become aware of your breathing. In addition to feeling and studying your bodily reactions as in all the other experiments, in this one sound is added, giving you one more dimension for judging the quality of your breathing. Because in our daily lives we are constantly interpreting sounds, it should be easy for you to judge quite precisely the sound quality of the sibilant "S." What was it like? Steady? Strong? Quavery? Weak? Would you consider it a good "S" sound or a poor one? Hence, was it a good breath or a poor one? If it was a good sound, enjoy it; feel what made it right as thoroughly as you would study a poorer sound. If it was not a good sound, try to feel what made it wrong. Maybe you pushed air out at the beginning or at the end of your exhalation, or both. Did your breath flow out evenly? Or did the sound quaver or fade out toward the end? If your hissing was too short or so soft that you could barely hear it, you can conclude that your exhalation was shallow and weak. In other words, the sound of your sibilant "S" is a true indication of the quality of your breathing. (By the way, a hissing radiator in the winter is a good example of the sound you should aim for.)

The Sibilant "S" Experiment also gives you an excellent opportunity to gauge the participation of your abdominal muscles in your breathing. Once in a while, place your hands on your lower abdomen when hissing and feel how much or how little your muscles are contracting during these exhalations. When you begin breathing work, you may find that the contractions of your muscles are not strong. But as you continue to do the experiments, you cannot miss feeling how much more vigorously your abdominal muscles will participate. Occasionally use your hands to feel whether your chest collapses or stays up, as it should, when you exhale on *ssss*.

The sibilant "S," being such a vigorous exhalation, eliminates large amounts of waste air. Therefore it is followed by deep inhalations, since the eliminated air has to be replaced. It is thus a strong stimulus to your breathing.

The Sibilant "S" Experiment is much more strenuous than the Straw and the Open Mouth experiments are. Because it is such an active procedure, I do not advise you to work with the Sibilant "S" Experiment when you are not feeling well. It requires more energy than you can or should apply in a weakened condition.

The Sibilant "S" Experiment will enliven your entire breathing apparatus and force you away from shallow breathing. In a short while you will feel reenergized, full of pep, raring to deal with your day's activities.

15

The Exhalation on the Palm Experiment

Having gained experience through the preceding experiments, you are now able to begin this one without disturbing your breathing. You may therefore start by using your exhalation from its very beginning instead of delaying until your exhalation has already begun. However, should you find that you are still disturbing your breathing before or when beginning, then continue as long as necessary to start the experiment after an average exhalation has begun to flow.

Holding your palm vertically, fairly close to your mouth, let a single exhalation through your mouth waft gently onto your palm as you make a soft, barely audible, continuous *haaaa* sound (*ha* as in "harbor"). (See Figure 13.)

This is not such an unfamiliar way of exhaling as it may seem. We breathe this way to clean our eyeglasses or a mirror, when we push the air out quickly and forcefully to produce maximum moisture. For this experiment do not push the air out; rather, try to let your breath stream out of your mouth slowly, as gently and steadily as possible, and only as long as the air streams out with ease. Try at the same time to leave your throat wide

Figure 13. Exhalation on the Palm Experiment.

open, without any pressure on it. As with the Straw Experiment, do not bend down, but raise your palm close to your mouth so you can remain upright easily when you work.

Your exhalations on *Haaaa* will be so soft and gentle that you will barely feel the rush of breath on your palm. But you will feel humidity and temperature distinctly. And, as with the Straw Experiment, you will feel your exhalations becoming gradually warmer as you continue. As in all experiments, take the time necessary to give the consequences of the stimulus to your breathing a chance to develop. Do not repeat the experiment until you feel that your breathing has become even again.

This experiment offers a particularly gentle way to increase your exhalations and thus induce deeper inhalations. In our noisy world you will find that this slight, barely audible *haaaa* sound is oddly restful. It not only affects your breathing, steadying it and making it fuller, but your total being is under its influence. When ending, you will find yourself in a delightful state of calm and ease.

16

The Skinfold Experiment

The quality of your breathing will improve so rapidly through breathing work that you will become aware—sometimes quite suddenly—that your chest cage is not at all elastic enough to accommodate comfortably your now considerably fuller breaths. Your chest cage will feel stiff, not expanding as much as your inhalations now require. And expand it should, in various directions—up, down, forward, and backward! But instead of facilitating your exhalations, your chest cage has become an obstacle, and deeper inhalations have to struggle so hard to get through that they become strangled in the process. They have become shallower and so are unable to reach full efficiency. The purpose of the Skinfold Experiment and of the following pressure experiments is to overcome this curtailing of your inhalations caused by the reduced elasticity of your chest cage.

A skinfold, as the name conveys, is a fold of skin, in fact a double layer, skin and underlying (subcutaneous) tissue. You get hold of a skinfold by grasping a portion of skin with your thumb and index finger or with your thumb and four other fingers. You may also grasp a skinfold with both hands simultaneously and from any direction that is easy for you—

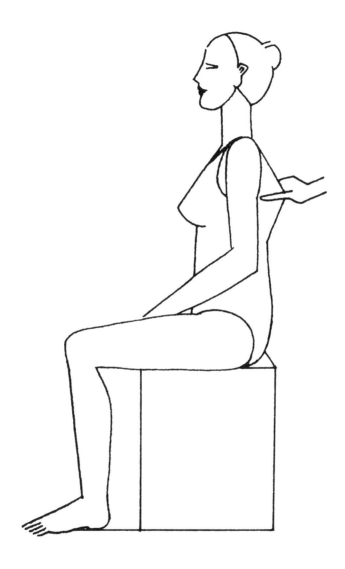

Figure 14. A skinfold.

horizontally, vertically, or diagonally. Hold the skinfold firmly, but do not pinch it.

A skinfold is grasped, lifted, and held off its base until a deeper breath gets through; then it is released. Lift the skinfold just barely off your chest cage in a direction away from the center of your body—that is, approximately forward in front, laterally on the sides, and backward from the back (Figure 14).

How does the Skinfold Experiment work? It has the same effect as when you open up a too-tight belt or brassiere after having worn it for a good while—you immediately expand and draw a deep breath of relief when you get free. That is exactly what will happen when you do the Skinfold Experiment. Only this time the problem is not a piece of clothing you have been wearing too tightly; you have been wearing *yourself* too tightly, if I may say so!

Skinfolds should be lifted off the chest cage from the front, the sides, and the back.

As with all experiments, work over one specific area for quite some time before starting on the next one.

I. SKINFOLDS OFF THE LOWER FRONT OF THE RIB CAGE

These are skinfolds grasped from the front of the chest cage (area 6 in Figure 10). All skinfolds should be lifted from your lowest ribs, not from your stomach. If you have any doubts about where your lowest ribs are located, trace the rim of your chest cage with your fingers, from the breastbone downward along your side and back. Only close to your spine do muscles hide this rim from your touch.

You can grasp a skinfold during any phase of your breathing. Hold it off for a few moments until a deeper inhalation sets in. Release the skinfold gently with this inhalation so as not to interfere with the incoming breath. Never let the skinfold slip from your fingers with a sudden snap. This would shock your breathing and undo all the good you may have derived from lifting it off.

Lift the same skinfold several times until you get a satisfactory reaction.

Move on only when strong reactions abate. For the next skinfold, grasp half of the former and half of the adjacent area of skin. Continue in this way above the rim of your chest cage from front to side. As before, give yourself the time needed to let all your reactions to the stimulus through and let your breathing level off before you grasp the next skinfold.

Leave out any areas where you are too tender or so tight that you cannot get hold of a skinfold. Move on to where you can grasp a skinfold painlessly. Should you have trouble grasping a skinfold from one direction, try from another one. You may grasp and lift a skinfold from any direction—horizontally, vertically, or diagonally—and with as many fingers as you like. Choose the easiest manner.

II. SKINFOLDS OFF THE SIDE OF THE RIB CAGE

Apply the same technique over your side (area 3 in Figure 10). Of course, *leave out the armpit*. It is easiest to start lifting skinfolds from the bottom of the chest cage and move gradually upward, on either horizontal or vertical paths.

The tissues on the sides of your rib cage may be tender, so use your fingers carefully. Try to grasp the skinfolds as gently as you can. If certain spots are too tender to be grasped or lifted, postpone them and try again later. Sometimes such areas do not ease up enough to permit skinfolds to be grasped until your back has been worked through with skinfolds.

Follow the same procedure as in the earlier experiments; after one side has been loosened up, compare its condition with the opposite side. Be open-minded. Sides can differ in tenderness and in the way they respond. Let all your reactions develop fully before you take another skinfold.

After having mastered the skill and gathered experience, you may lift skinfolds simultaneously on the right and left, either in the front or on the sides. This is a highly efficient way to recuperate quickly during the day when there is little time. It will speedily improve your breathing proficiency and thus restore your energy.

Lifting skinfolds simultaneously right and left from either your front or your sides near the bottom of your rib cage can be of help in overcoming hiccups. As these areas are so close to the diaphragm, the latter, more often than not, will ease up sufficiently, together with your chest cage. As soon as the cramping of the diaphragm lets up, your hiccups will stop.

III. SKINFOLDS OFF THE BACK

Skinfolds from the back (area 4 in Figure 10) should be lifted in the same manner as all others. But in the back, do not work only over your chest cage; you should also include the small of the back, the area between your lowest ribs and your pelvis—that is, you lift skinfolds all over your back down to the pelvic rim.

For this work on your back, you need a helper. Show that person, using the skin on the back of your hand, what a skinfold is and how it should be lifted, held, and released slowly. Your helper should begin by trying out where he or she can best start working with you, as people differ greatly in looseness and tenderness between the shoulder and the small of the back. Your helper should start where you are most comfortable with the skinfold grip, working either down from the shoulder or up from the rim of the pelvis. Of course, all areas where you are too tight or too tender should be skipped until later.

Be forewarned that there may be large areas of the back where you find yourself too tight for a skinfold to be gripped. Eventually, of course, there will be no tightness or tenderness at all in your back, and skinfolds may be lifted comfortably anywhere. I should add that there are innumerable people who never have difficulties with the lifting of skinfolds.

Plan a half hour or more for working on your back. Do not pity your helper for spending that precious time on you. His or her breathing will be affected as much as yours. Your helper may also yawn, stretch, and draw deep, satisfying breaths. Moreover, it is fascinating to observe the reactions of the person with whom you are working. These reactions are clearly visible in your back. If your helper is not able to see them, he or she should put a hand over the area where a skinfold has been taken and try to feel the reactions underneath. The hand should rest lightly on your back so as not to interfere with the expansion of your rib cage.

70

Whenever a skinfold has been lifted off its base, be open-minded to any kind of breathing reaction that may come, as well as to any bodily changes that may occur. An urge to wiggle and lengthen your whole trunk may well ensue and should be let through freely. You may have to yawn unexpectedly often. You will feel your chest cage open up pleasantly, accommodating your deeper breaths with ease.

Before changing to the other half of your back, compare your two halves, the one that has been worked through and the one that has not yet been worked on. Remain alert to your reactions as you work on the other half of your back. Will your reactions be similar, or will they be different?

Though tenderness may hamper your work occasionally in the beginning, lifting skinfolds is a particularly pleasant way of working. My students are fond of this experiment, especially of the work over their backs. It is such a relief to be helped rather than to have to do for oneself! The easy expansion of the chest cage for all the deeper breaths that the experiment provokes feels so utterly satisfying and gives relief from unnecessary strain.

This is an experiment that clearly demonstrates the interdependence of the way our breathing functions with our total physical, mental, and emotional condition. You will become aware of striking changes not only in your breathing but in your muscle tone as well. You will find yourself relaxing or toning up; you will notice the change in your carriage, the different quality of your movements, and all the relief of strains going along with the changes in your breathing. Your bodily ease makes for a calmer mood. You may feel as though heavy burdens have been lifted from you; decisions will come easily, and you will face the future with confidence.

Response to this experiment is generally so instantaneous and so thorough that you can, when in need, use it to restore your breathing and your equilibrium in a very short time. If you become tired, suffer a shock, or are overcome by sudden stage fright, lifting a few skinfolds simultaneously from the front or both sides of your chest cage will make your breathing recover. In a few moments you will be ready to resume your activities with full efficiency.

17

The Pressure Experiments

It is always useful to have more than one approach to solve a problem, and so the pressure experiments offer another way to increase the elasticity of your rib cage. As your breathing continues to become fuller, the need for greater elasticity of your rib cage persists. After your preparation through the Skinfold Experiment, you are ready to try the pressure experiments. Pressure—of course, very light pressure—is another means of regaining the needed elasticity of the chest cage.

The use of pressure may sound strange. Let me explain. We all know how a down pillow rebounds into shape after we get up from it. The human chest cage reacts similarly. It also fills out after an applied pressure has been released. But the chest cage not only returns to its former constricted shape; pressure, being a stimulus, makes it expand more fully than before. The diaphragm, being attached to the lower ribs, will then have a wider span and, consequently, will work more efficiently. Relief from a stiff and narrow chest cage makes your breathing easier, more efficient, and definitely more enjoyable.

The pressure experiments call for light fingertip pressure applied over the whole chest cage, on the breastbone as well as on and between the ribs.

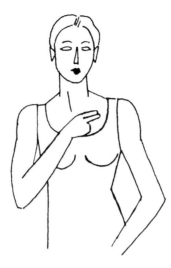

Figure 15. Fingertip pressure.

Here I will describe the pressure experiments in their entirety. However, I advise you not to do them one right after another. You will feel a need for a change in stimulus after having worked with pressure on the breast-bone and on the ribs before continuing with pressure between the ribs. If so, change to one or more of the previous experiments with which you have worked successfully and take up the Pressure Between the Ribs Experiment later. By then you will again be fully receptive to the pressure stimulus.

Contrary to tapping (see Chapter 12), which can safely be done all over the chest cage in one session, pressure, though applied lightly, being a much stronger stimulus, should be used in only one area at a time. Apply pressure either to your breastbone, the upper front of your chest, on your sides, or on your back. I would advise you to work repeatedly over a particular area before taking on another one. If any spot or a whole area feels tender, skip it and press there later, when you have worked through the sur-rounding areas. By then, the tender areas will have eased up and will take pressure without discomfort.

Pressure is a strong stimulus to breathing. Therefore limit the time and work only as long as you feel comfortable. One can tolerate only a certain amount of stimulation and change in one's breathing. Too much stimulation will bring an intensity of reactions that will overwhelm rather than benefit you. Should you ever feel that you have done too much, stop. Wait before continuing, until your breathing has returned to a calm state.

I. PRESSURE ON THE BREASTBONE

Start the Pressure on the Breastbone (sternum) Experiment (area 5 in Figure 10). If you are not sure how far your breastbone extends, trace it with your fingertips before beginning. Feel where the breastbone begins and where it ends so that you do not press by mistake above your breastbone into the neck, or below into the pit of your stomach.

As before, begin by feeling when your exhalations and your inhalations occur. Shortly after an ordinary exhalation has begun, press gently on your breastbone, using the fingertips of one or both hands—the index and third finger used together are best. Release the pressure with the next inhalation. Since the breastbone is narrow, keep your fingers close together or you may by mistake press your ribs instead of just your breastbone.

Start the experiment at the upper end of the breastbone. Press gently but firmly, as if you intended to test the elasticity of the bone. Release the pressure slowly with the incoming inhalation. Do not let your fingers snap off suddenly, as that would disturb your breathing.

Gradually apply pressure all the way down the length of the breastbone. If you encounter tender spots, move farther down and come back to them later. Their tenderness may disappear quickly during the same work period, or it may take a few more days of applying pressure above and below these spots.

When you have a cold, and even for some time afterward, the breastbone area may be quite tender to the touch. Then press very lightly, or, if you have not yet had much experience with the pressure experiments, postpone them for a few days until there is no more tenderness.

Pressure on the breastbone has proved helpful in avoiding the congestion of the bronchi that often follows colds. You may then cough up a great deal of phlegm.

Asthmatics can benefit greatly from this experiment. They, of course, must be particularly careful to proceed slowly, as they can only gradually tolerate more elasticity of their chest cages. They must make absolutely certain that their breathing has become even before applying the next pressure stimulus.

In all pressure experiments, try to feel not only where your fingertips touch—the surface of your body—but try to feel from the center of your body outward toward the pressing fingers. This will facilitate your reactions.

After you have released the pressure, be sure to allow enough time—first, for all the breathing responses to break through, and then, for your breathing to become fully even again. As with the Skinfold Experiment, work on the same spot a number of times. Move on only when your reactions have lessened considerably. The best way to move farther down on the breastbone is by pressing with your fingertips half on the area you have pressed before and half on a new area.

The upper part of the breastbone is not very elastic and cannot give in much to pressure. But even so, the lightest pressure on this area is extremely stimulating to breathing. Farther down on your breastbone, you can feel more of a true give to the pressure of your fingertips. Press particularly gently in this area.

Breathing reactions to this experiment are usually very strong, almost dramatic. You may have to yawn innumerable times, may get enormously deep breaths that may penetrate with great urgency, and it may take you much longer than you anticipated to let your breathing become even.

The results of this experiment are extraordinarily rewarding. Breaths become deep and full, filling out the upper chest, raising and keeping the breastbone up, thus helping to overcome poor posture. A student once described her condition by saying, "It feels like an iron vise has been taken off the front of my chest!" The sensations of the breath pouring into the front of the chest cage unimpeded and of the breastbone area yielding with as much elasticity as needed give a feeling of tremendous relief.

II. PRESSURE ON THE RIBS

The ribs are even more decisive for the elasticity of the chest cage than the breastbone. The following experiments promote the elasticity of the ribs and make their full and easy expansion available for your by now much more vigorous breathing.

Pressure on the ribs should not be applied until you have had experience with the use and effects of pressure on the breastbone, and thus have already prepared the rib cage for more elasticity.

Pressure should be applied on one area at a time: first on the ribs of the upper front of your chest cage, then on the ribs of the lower front, and finally on the ribs of your sides and on the ribs of your back.

PRESSURE ABOVE THE BREAST

Apply to the ribs of the upper front of your chest cage area (area 1 in Figure 10) the same kind of fingertip pressure that you used on your breastbone. Begin on the first rib, the one you can feel just below your collarbone. Start close to the breastbone and apply pressure along the rib toward the side. Part of the upper ribs are obscured by the breast muscles. Apply pressure on them in the same direction until you reach your shoulder joint. The ribs respond to pressure applied on the covering muscles. Press during exhalation, gently but firmly, and release the pressure slowly at the beginning of the following inhalation. All doubts as to when to release the pressure will soon disappear because the inhalation air will flow in so forcefully that it will throw your fingers off, whether you intended to release the pressure or not. And you will not have to be reminded to wait after applying pressure until your breathing has become even. You will feel not only the agitation of your breathing but also the need to wait until your breaths flow calmly out and in again before reapplying pressure.

Gradually press along as many ribs as you can feel *above* your breast. *Never press on the breast itself.* As before, postpone pressure on all tender areas. Try them later during the same session or after a few sessions. The tenderness will be relieved, and the area can be pressed without giving discomfort.

When you compare sides after having pressed on the upper half of the chest cage on one side, you will become aware of startling differences. For example, you may feel as though you breathed only in the particular area of the upper chest on which you applied the pressure. The other side may feel almost lifeless, as if no breathing were taking place in it at all. If you have advanced that far, it is time to change and apply pressure to the opposite side of your upper chest cage.

PRESSURE BELOW THE BREAST

Pressure should be applied on the lower front ribs, the ones from below the breast to the bottom of the rib cage (area 6 in Figure 10). Before starting, trace with your fingertips the rim of the lowest ribs so that you are sure how far down your rib cage extends.

Proceed on the lower ribs as you did on the upper ones. Press with your fingertips along each rib from middle to side.

As you work with pressure on the ribs in the front of your rib cage, you may be in for a surprise. Though the stimulus is given on the front part of the ribs, you will occasionally feel a strong breathing response not only in this area, as you would expect, but also in the back of your chest cage. Ribs react in their totality, along their entire span, which winds from front to spine. Therefore, though you apply pressure only in the front, you will find the whole half of your chest cage responding.

Be particularly gentle and careful with the pressure on the lowest ribs because they are so close to the diaphragm. And be prepared to find these ribs tender in certain spots.

Your reactions to the pressure on the lowest ribs may be particularly rewarding. You may need more time than usual between pressure applications to let all reactions fully through and until an even way of breathing reestablishes itself. Be open-minded and let your breathing respond in any way it will, from yawning, to heaving, to sighing, to an impulse to wriggle or to stretch, to drawing immensely deep breaths. Give your breathing a chance to benefit as much as possible from the stimulus. But as pressure is a particularly strong stimulus to breathing, be careful not to work longer than you can tolerate comfortably. Otherwise you may easily encounter too much of an upheaval. However, if you follow this advice, you will achieve increased elasticity and eventually the unhampered widening of your rib cage. The sensations of no longer being confined and of no longer being forced to labor to accommodate fuller breaths will give you great relief— relief that makes this experiment an especially gratifying one.

PRESSURE ON THE SIDES

Next apply pressure on each rib along the side of the chest cage (area 3 in Figure 10). Proceed in the same way you did with the ribs in the front. Start with the lowest rib. It is the easiest to press on and usually the least tender. Work gradually upward along the ribs on one side. Later, work on your other side. Apply pressure from front to back, from where you stopped working in the front to where your back begins. *Do not press into the armpit.* Press only over one-half of your chest cage so that you can make a comparison checkup with the other half before applying pressure to it.

Many people do not make much use of their sides for breathing and may find—and this is the proof—that they are quite tender to the touch in large areas. That is why it is advisable to start pressure on the side on the lowest rib and work gradually upward. If even the lowest ribs are too tender for very gentle pressure, omit this part of the pressure experiments for the time being. Try your sides again after a few more weeks of other breathing experiments. In fact, postpone this pressure as long as the area is sensitive. The easing up of the rib cage will happen gradually. So press on a rib farther up only if you can take the pressure comfortably. But not everybody is tender on the side of the rib cage. There are many who can apply pressure with ease on their sides right away.

PRESSURE ON THE BACK

Pressure on the ribs of the back (area 4 in Figure 10) is easiest to apply either sitting up or lying on your side or your stomach. Though you could work over a good part of your back by yourself, it feels and works particularly well if you have a helper. Sit or lie whichever way you are most comfortable. Begin yourself or have your helper begin with pressure on the lowest rib, moving from close to the spine toward the side of the body. Work slowly along each rib. When your helper reaches the shoulder blade, he or she should press on it instead of the ribs, and you will feel the ribs respond.

The change in the quality of your breathing through the pressure experiments will be quite extraordinary. Once a student was so overwhelmed that she announced in the middle of an experiment, "I feel just as if I unzipped a couple of ribs!"—a very apt description. The sense of tightness in your chest cage will have vanished, and in its place there will be feelings of immense elasticity, freedom, looseness, of having no obstacle to the expansion of your chest cage for breathing. You will not only breathe more fully, you will feel marvelously refreshed.

III. PRESSURE BETWEEN THE RIBS

Another major factor contributing greatly to the elasticity of your chest cage is the condition of the intercostal muscles (mm. intercostales), which extend in two layers between your ribs. They move your ribs together and apart with every breath you take. These muscles need proper tone to function well. If they are in a state of continuous overcontraction—as most people's are—the rib cage is decreased in size. The diaphragm, attached to the lowest ribs, thus has a smaller circumference and cannot work to its full potential. The intercostal muscles cannot function adequately, either. They cannot contract vigorously for exhalations, and they cannot comply sufficiently with the extension of the rib cage during inhalations. Thus curtailed, one's everyday breathing becomes habitually shallow. Consequently, no breaths are fully satisfying, and they are achieved by laboring instead of with ease.

Fingertip pressure, the same kind you applied on your ribs and in the same order, applied on these muscles—that is, into the spaces between your ribs (the intercostal spaces)—will greatly contribute to restoring their normal tone. Then they can contract and relax again with ease according to your needs.

Many of you will enjoy immediate and tremendously beneficial results—

79

vastly deeper breaths, spreading out of the rib cage, lengthening of the trunk—from this pressure stimulus. Your only "obstacle" may be that you change so much so rapidly in the areas you have pressed on that other parts of your rib cage may become uncomfortable and have to be attended to. A few pressures on the areas where they are needed will usually suffice and work can soon be resumed.

Some people, however, are extremely stiff in their intercostal muscles and therefore should work on them carefully and in short sessions. They should undertake longer periods only much later, after having gained experience with this particular stimulus and its effects, and after having become better acquainted with their own condition. People are quite unprepared to find a cramped, unyielding musculature where they might not have expected to have muscles at all!

Also, these intercostal muscles, having been in such limited use, may be rather tender to the touch. Wherever there is tenderness to pressure, proceed as you did with the other experiments: Stop and release the pressure immediately. Apply pressure on an adjoining spot instead. If the whole area is tender, postpone this experiment until your rib cage has become more elastic through other experiments.

Muscles between the ribs on your sides can be extremely tender. If that is so, reverse the order and work on your back first and on your sides later.

There is a fair chance that the intercostal muscles, not having been used freely enough for a long time, may react to sudden, more intensive use by becoming muscle-bound. If you feel somewhat stiff and achy in your trunk after having worked with this experiment, do not worry. You did nothing wrong, nor is anything wrong with you! Let the area rest for a few days, and continue the experiment when you are free of discomfort. In time, you will be able to enjoy fully the increased elasticity of your rib cage. The feeling of ease and freedom in your breathing will compensate for any distress suffered in achieving it.

As with the other experiments, let all your reactions through, including yawning and stretching, and enjoy the deeper breaths that will come to you. Take the time to let your breathing become fully even before reapplying pressure.

You will be amazed at how much the shape of your chest cage may change through the pressure experiments—in depth, from front to back as well as from side to side; and in length, from top to bottom. You may need to alter your clothes to accommodate your expanded rib cage.

This, too, is an experiment that should be done over a selected area for a long time before going on to the next one. Once in a while, breathing where pressure has been applied may extend the rib cage locally so much that other parts of the chest cage will have to be temporarily pressed to level off the difference.

During the day, when you have no time for extended work, use pressure between the ribs to recover quickly from fatigue or overstimulation. Once familiar with the process, your body will respond rapidly. Two or three light pressures on any area of intercostal space will be all that is needed to recuperate—maybe not fully, but enough to enable you to pursue your activities without undue strain. Press in the area of greatest need or wherever you know from experience that you will gain the quickest response.

18

The Position Experiments

In all the experiments you have now tried, it was the increase in breathing that brought about a greater expansion of your rib cage. In the position experiments this process is reversed. By passive expansion of the rib cage and of the diaphragm, achieved through positioning of your body, a greater animation of your breathing will result. The expansion is a passive one because you are not stretching yourself; instead, the position you take leads to the expansion that stimulates your breathing.

There are many positions useful for this purpose. I would like to introduce three that are especially conducive to fuller breathing.

I. TRUNK LEANING SIDEWAYS

Sitting cross-legged on the floor (if you are not comfortable sitting cross-legged, sit on a bench, or on a chair with another chair at your side), bend your trunk over sideways until your forearm rests on the floor (or bench, or chair), and remain for a while in this position (Figure 16). Move ex-

Figure 16. Trunk leaning sideways.

tremely slowly, testing at first how far over you can lean while remaining seated on your whole pelvis, though, of course, more body weight will rest on the half of the pelvis on the side toward which you are leaning. The hand of your supporting arm should rest on its back on the floor to facilitate your downward movement and to avoid pushing you unintentionally off the floor or impeding the easy bending of your elbow.

Wherever you feel resistance to the movement through stiffness or aching, tap yourself (with the same firm tap mentioned in Chapter 8) to help your muscles ease up and to better accommodate your movement. Remain in the leaning position for a while—regardless of how far you are able to lean over—and feel how the position affects your breathing. Give in to the expansion of your outer side, your flank, as best you can. Let all your breathing reactions develop fully, whatever they may be. You may experience at this point the whole range of what are by now familiar reactions in your breathing, from emergency responses to deep, satisfying breaths.

At first remain in the leaning position for short periods only. Later, when you are fully comfortable in this position, you may lean for quite a while, accommodating and enjoying the reactions of your breathing as it becomes more and more stimulated through the position. If you feel achy, tap yourself when leaning over, when moving, and also when sitting up again. Always balance slowly and carefully back to your starting position, making sure to let all responses fully through that follow your return to the sitting position.

Do not be discouraged if you cannot immediately lean far over sideways. Actually, even the least inclination of your trunk will have a tremendous effect on your breathing. You will be surprised at how rapidly you will succeed in leaning farther and farther until your forearm reaches the floor (or whatever support you have chosen). You will soon be able to remain in this leaning position longer, so that you have ample time to let all responses in your breathing develop and spread through your body.

Begin the experiment by leaning over sideways in whatever is the most comfortable direction for you. Eventually, lean in the plane of your trunk— that is, absolutely sideways, not slightly forward as you may have done in the beginning.

It will give you great satisfaction to do a comparison checkup on your breathing now after having leaned over toward one side only. You will feel once more, as you have in previous experiments, the sensation of breathing predominantly in the area of your chest cage engaged in the experiment—in this case, the half of your chest cage that has been expanded. Your breaths will feel full and deep, and will fill this half of your chest cage with ease. The other half of your trunk may feel not only unparticipating but also narrow and confining to your breathing.

Having achieved this marked difference between the two halves of your chest cage, you are ready to change direction and lean over toward your other side.

Later, when you become so comfortable in this position that there is not enough of a challenge, you may increase the demands of the position by taking the arm of your outer side into the movement, raising it all the way upward, close to your head.

II. LEANING FORWARD ON ELBOWS

Sitting cross-legged on the floor (or on a chair with a low table in front of you), lean with your trunk forward until your bent elbows rest on the floor (or table). Support your head in your hands and remain in this position for a while (Figure 17). Let yourself ease up, give in to the lengthening and widening of your trunk, and, most important of all, let your breathing respond to this position in any way it may.

This is a comfortable position, though not easily achieved by everybody at first try, and remaining in it for a while may seem impossible at first. You may wonder how you will ever get your elbows on the floor (or table). But this is not as difficult as it may seem. If you cannot get all the way down with your elbows, put a stack of newspapers or books in front of you to provide a support higher than the floor (or table). As with the leaning-sideward position, any forward inclination of the trunk, even the slightest, will make your chest cage expand and stimulate your breathing. Rest in this position, regardless of how far down you get, and let all reactions in

Figure 17. Leaning forward on elbows.

your breathing through. Stay a reasonable length of time—not too long for the first few attempts—and return to an upright position slowly and carefully. Tap where and when you may need it to relieve stiffness or achiness. Gradually lower your support, a bit at a time. When you can get farther down, try to rest one, then the other, elbow on your thigh. Still later, try to rest both elbows simultaneously on your thighs. Then try to rest one and then the other elbow on the floor (or table). (See Figure 18.) After a while, you will find that resting with both elbows on the floor or table has become quite easy and an utterly comfortable position, highly stimulating to your breathing. Take your time, do not be overambitious, and do not force yourself into the position. If you were stiff in the beginning, you will limber up gradually.

The more you are at ease in this position, the more your breathing will respond. The loosening up of the whole torso is a strong and pleasant stimulus to breathing. You will feel deeper and deeper breaths fill your chest cage. Your lower back area will open up particularly extensively for breathing. As a result, you will be supplied with more energy and a sense of well-being. Your breathing will give you full support. My students often assume this easing-up position before class to get themselves ready for work.

III. KNEELING WITH TRUNK FORWARD

Kneel, sit down on your feet, and let your trunk rest on your legs, either with your forehead on the floor or your head turned sideways, arms resting on the floor at your sides (Figure 19). Should you not be able to sit on your feet, put a pillow on your calves and sit down on the pillow to do the experiment. Gradually lower yourself until you are sitting on your feet. Stay for a while in this position, letting all the reactions in your breathing through that this position provokes. Raise yourself extremely slowly, sit back on your feet, and feel yourself. Have you changed? In what way? What is your general condition? Are you perhaps less cramped, or less flabby? What does your breathing feel like? Compare the impression of your condition now with the one you received from your first checkup, which you took care of as usual before starting. Do not hesitate to take all the time you may need

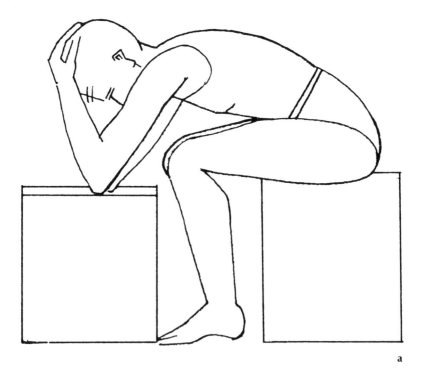

a

Figure 18. Ways to achieve the forward leaning position.

b

c

d

Figure 19. A good resting position, favorable to breathing.

to feel yourself and to become aware of changes in your condition. Where are you still unresponsive, or not responding enough? Where and in what way are you responding best?

Repeat this position experiment a number of times, always allowing yourself to be changed as much as possible in your breathing as well as in your general bodily condition.

Of course, tap yourself whenever you feel a need for it, as you did during the other position experiments. Kneel on a blanket if your knees or feet are uncomfortable in this position.

You may change, if you like, the position of your arms and let them rest stretched out forward on the floor instead of at your sides.

This kneeling position is not only restful, giving your whole body a chance to ease up, but of great benefit to your breathing. The feeling of ample breathing in your lower back is particularly satisfying. Your trunk will have eased up and, being more lengthened and widened, will now be ready to yield with much more elasticity to your breathing needs.

Individuals vary so much in elasticity or stiffness that it is impossible to say with which of these three position experiments you should begin. Try each one a few times; then start work with the position that is easiest for you and best facilitates reactions.

Once you have experience with these three positions, you can also use them as a means for quick recovery of your breathing as well as for your general recovery. Even if you take them just once, and briefly, you will be reminded to let necessary changes through.

You will feel the difference in your bodily functioning immediately. You will be less hypertense or less flaccid, your spirits will be lifted, and your breathing will support you fully.

19

The Humming Experiment

Sounds for speaking and singing are made by using the air of the exhalation with simultaneous activation of our vocal folds (vocal cords). As exhalations are so decisively involved in the production of sounds, making sounds can also serve effectively as breathing experiments. In addition, exhalations with use of the vocal folds afford more energy than exhalations without sound. Consequently, the use of sound helps to energize breathing and is therefore a good way to help your breathing recuperate from sluggishness. In all these experiments with sounds, there are two factors at your disposal for judging the quality of your breathing: your body awareness and your hearing.

You hum by letting an exhalation stream out through your nose, lips closed, and using your vocal folds to produce the humming *mmmmm* sound. Be careful not to prolong your sound by pressing or forcing the air out, and don't worry about your pitch—any pitch will do. Let the humming *mmmmm* sound stream for as long as it may. Try not to force it or curtail it. Always feel yourself when humming and listen to the sound. Are you comfortable when humming? Is just a puff of air escaping, making only a short humming possible? How long can you hum without forcing your breath? Aim for a long, steady, vibrating *mmmmm* sound. Remember the Don Cossack choir—it used perfect humming sounds.

Later on, when you find your humming satisfactory, you may begin to try humming on different pitches, higher and lower ones. Feel where the resonance of your sounds is emphasized. Is it more in your head or more in your chest?

Beginning the humming a moment after an average exhalation has begun will make it easier for you to achieve a pressureless, unexplosive, steady, and pleasant *mmmmm* sound. You will achieve a vibrating sound quality much faster than if you began to hum at the very beginning of your exhalation. Eventually, with experience, you may begin to hum at the beginning of an exhalation.

After each humming, wait for its effect on the quality of the breathing that follows. You will probably draw a few extraordinarily deep and enjoyable breaths. Maybe you will have to yawn several times before you regain an average way of breathing. This "average way" will undoubtedly be of a better quality than the breathing you became aware of during your checkup at the beginning. Try not to interfere with any of your responses. Consciously give in to them. Take your time and do not rush into a new hum. Instead, give yourself a while to rest and to let the different way of breathing that follows your humming settle in before giving a new stimulus to your breathing by repeating the experiment.

Making sounds is such a pleasant way of working that you will enjoy doing this experiment both frequently and for long periods of time. The more satisfactory your sounds, the fuller your exhalations become and the deeper your inhalations will be. That means, of course, that you have achieved a more efficient way of breathing.

When your humming has become steady, strong, and vibrating, you may vary the sound by adding vowels to it. Begin with a hum, then add a vowel, and let your breath sound as long as it flows freely. Vary the vowels: *ma*, with *a* as in "palm"; *ma*, with *a* as in "name"; *me*, with *e* as in "beet"; *mo*, with *o* as in "over"; or *mu*, with the *u* sound as in "pool." If you feel up to it, and adventurous, too, you may combine two or more vowels after your humming *m*: *mua, mue, muoa,* and so on. You can play with sounds in many ways.

It is important not to force or press, but to let your breath flow freely. Remember, start out on any pitch and eventually use higher and lower pitches.

Humming with added vowels is not only fun but makes you feel and hear your breath distinctly, so that you become aware of its strength or weakness as well as of any poor habits you may have developed in the use of your voice. Teachers, actors, singers, and musicians have greatly profited from these experiments. Your ordinary speaking voice will markedly improve. Voices tend to become fuller, more resonant, carry better, and are often considerably deeper in pitch.

Amuse yourself sometimes by humming with an added vowel when you hear a loud noise—a roaring train, or a plane flying overhead, for instance. Can you still hear your voice? Or has it been drowned out by the noise? This is a good check on the state of your breathing and will help you ascertain whether you are low or high on energy.

20

The Movement Experiments

Generally speaking, movements are stimulating to breathing if we let our breathing adapt and do not interfere with the necessary adjustments of breathing to our activities. Our breathing then gives us adequate support automatically. I am referring, of course, to normal daily activities. Specialized activities, such as those required in certain kinds of work—some sports, moving furniture, singing, acting, dancing, the playing of wind instruments—present an extraordinary challenge to breathing. Instead of using the support of our breathing, most of us interfere with it when becoming active. Observe people's breathing when they lift a telephone receiver, when they brush their teeth or hair, when they bend over, or when they climb stairs.

But why observe only others? Feel yourself during movements! You will be amazed at how much you hinder your breath—by holding it, pressing on it, inhaling actively instead of letting the breath flow in freely by itself, to mention only a few of the many ways in which you probably disturb your breathing when moving. You thus rob yourself of what should be the most effective support for movement. Not only do you lose support, you create obstacles. This diminished supply of energy as a consequence of poor breathing makes work and life exhausting. And how exhilarating life could be!

Even the intention of moving may provoke an interference with breathing. It is surprising how many people hold their breath before starting a movement. You will be increasingly aware of doing this yourself as you become more familiar with your breathing. At the very moment that you need an ample oxygen supply and adequate elimination of carbon dioxide, you will find yourself thwarting the process, an upsetting experience. Once you become aware of this habit, most movements—or any other action, for that matter—seem to involve a preliminary holding of the breath.

Becoming aware of how you hamper your breathing as soon as you contemplate an action or just barely begin one will probably trouble you. Moving will seem a strain instead of a pleasure. But being aware of the many ways in which you can and do disturb your breathing and make your life hard is the first step in the process of freeing yourselves from these interferences. Only if you are aware that something is wrong can you try to do something about it. The following experiments will show how movements can be beneficial instead of exhausting to your breathing.

I. ARM STRETCH SITTING OR STANDING

NOTE ON STRETCHING: Unlike the urge to stretch described in Chapter 7, the following experiments use a deliberate stretch, one started on purpose, to attain a stimulation of breathing.

Sitting with your hands in your lap, or *standing* with your arms at your sides, move one arm upward. Do not raise it stiffly, but use all its joints. Bend your arm until your hand is at shoulder level. Then unfold your arm. Choose any direction you like for this movement. Hesitate for a moment when your arm has reached its full length; then stretch your arm, elongating it ever so slightly (Figure 20).

Move slowly throughout; the stretch should be gentle, not a recklessly executed movement. To achieve such a light stretch after your arm has unfolded, make a grasping movement with your fingers, as if you wanted to

Figure 20. Arm stretch, standing.

get hold of something just a trifle beyond your reach. Stretch out for an instant only, then release your arm and return your hand to your lap (or side), again using all joints freely. Finally, let your arm rest.

Be careful not to raise, stiffen, or strain your shoulder during the moment of stretching. Be sure to let your arm react through all its joints—fingers, wrist, elbow, shoulder—and try to let the stretch penetrate into your whole trunk.

Not immediately, but gradually, your ability to react to the stretch will increase. You will feel yourself strongly affected all the way through into your pelvis, when sitting, or down to your feet, when standing. Allow your body and your breathing to respond freely. A lengthening of your trunk, yawning, and deep breaths will follow. The general toning up of your body resulting from this kind of stretching will sustain the better way of breathing you will have achieved.

By changing the direction of your movements, you can vary the directions in which the stretching will affect you.

This experiment is so effective that it will have a far-reaching influence on your everyday life. There are so many times during the day when you need to stretch to reach an object. Instead of straining yourself, you will welcome and enjoy the opportunities to stretch and benefit through such otherwise dreaded tasks as cleaning the bathtub, scrubbing the floor, or plucking a can from a high shelf.

II. ARM STRETCH LYING

Lying on your stomach, place one arm diagonally ahead of you on the floor (Figure 21). If this position feels awkward or uncomfortable, move your arm farther down—if need be, all the way down to shoulder level. It is essential to start in a comfortable position. Stretch your arm in the direction in which it is lying by creeping with your fingertips over the floor as far out as you can without straining yourself. Grip the floor with your fingertips. Hold on for a moment, so that you have time to give in to the stretch and let yourself expand and your breathing respond. One way to accomplish this is to try to become comfortable in the elongated position by letting yourself settle on the floor. Eventually, release the grip of your

Figure 21. Arm stretch, lying on stomach.

fingers, so that you ease out from the stretch. Rest a moment and feel what changes the stretch may have induced in your breathing and in the general condition of your body. Be accommodating as long as you are still changing. Then rest for a while to let all these changes settle in. When you feel that an even manner of breathing has reestablished itself, you are ready for another stimulus and may stretch once more.

This stretching can be varied by gradually placing your arm farther upward on the floor until you finally stretch with your arm close to your head.

Should your arm or any other part of your body be achy, interrupt your stretching, bend your elbow, and move your arm down close to your body. Then use a firm tap to relieve the discomfort. Few people's necks are limber enough to permit them to lie for any length of time flat on their stomachs with their heads turned sideways. Therefore turn your head once in a while to the other side to avoid a kink in the neck. If necessary, rub the back of your neck to ease strained muscles.

When you begin this stretching experiment, do not work for long periods. A few attempts at stretching may be all that you can take in the beginning. Above all, do not force yourself into an uncomfortable position; the stretch should always be a pleasant one. Stretching, once you are limber enough, will not only *feel* good, it will *do* good. Your breathing will be greatly stimulated. Your trunk, elongated and widened through stretching, will accommodate with ease your much fuller breathing, and your breathing will sustain the fuller quality in subsequent breaths for quite some time.

III. LEG STRETCH

Lie down *on your back*, both legs at full length on the floor; or, if that position is somewhat uncomfortable, pull one leg up, bend it, and place your foot on the floor close to your pelvis. Leading with your heel (your foot bent to avoid cramps), stretch your extended leg slightly (Figure 22). Hold the stretch for a moment and let all reactions to the stretching—in general bodily condition and in your breathing—through. Gently and slowly release the stretch and give yourself time to let the aftereffects of the stretch pervade you.

Figure 22. Leg stretch, lying on back.

During the stretching, make sure that your pelvis remains firmly anchored, lying level on the floor. In other words, make sure you do not mistake a lengthening of your leg caused by a movement of your pelvis with a true stretch through all the joints of your leg. As with your arm, stretch lightly and gently, allowing the stretching to penetrate into your trunk. Do not force the movement. The aim is not to stretch particularly far, but to be affected by even the smallest reaching out.

Your reactions may be delayed at first; later on, they will be instantaneous. Proceed to the next stretching movement only after you have taken enough time to let even delayed reactions through, and after you have rested awhile to let these changes in your breathing and in your body become stabilized. Among the changes you may experience are resting with your whole body more firmly on the floor, an easing up in your joints, and deeper exhalations and inhalations. Before stretching your other leg, do a comparison checkup. Feel how your breathing and the total state of the half of your body you worked with compares with that of the other half.

The same kind of stretch can be done *lying on your stomach*. Stretch one leg slightly, pointing your toes. Should your foot not be elastic enough and tend to cramp, stretch your leg with your foot bent, leading with the sole.

When you have gained some experience and can tolerate a stronger stimulus, you may also stretch not only one but both arms or both legs, and eventually stretch arms and legs simultaneously.

You will discover that these stretching movements, executed with emphasis on your breathing responses, are not only a grand means of restoring your breathing to better functioning but also a means of supporting a bodily condition that will enable you to sustain recuperation. You will find that you have plenty of energy at your disposal and that you can cope with many of life's daily irritations with little stress.

IV. A SPECIAL ARM MOVEMENT

Lie on your side on the floor, legs stretched or slightly bent, whichever you prefer. Make sure that your trunk and pelvis are exactly balanced on your side. Do not tilt forward or backward. Leaning might make you slump

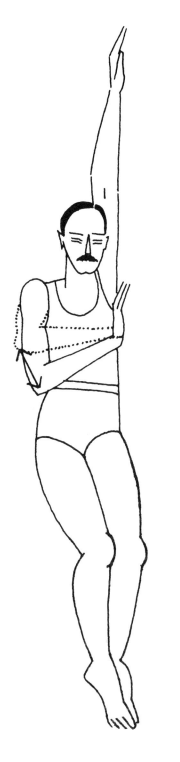

Figure 23. Special arm movement.

and roll over. Having to balance will keep you from ever becoming flabby when you ease up during the course of the experiment. Using the uppermost arm, place the palm on the floor in front of your chest, fairly close to your body, elbow bent, fingertips pointing somewhat toward you. Leading with your elbow, turn your arm slightly upward—in the direction of your head—yielding in your wrist and shoulder joint (Figure 23). Hold your arm for a moment in the turned position and then let it sink back into the position from which you started. Move extremely slowly, making the smallest effort possible. Feel yourself during and after moving. Try to let all your responses through, regardless of sequence or timing. You may at first feel compelled to change your position on the floor, to stretch your trunk farther out, to change the position of your legs by placing your knees farther up or down on the floor, or to let your rib cage settle closer to the floor. You may feel an immediate response to each movement in your breathing, or your reactions may be somewhat delayed. It is not important which reactions penetrate first and which later. Some may happen simultaneously.

Most often, though, as you experiment with this movement, you will feel that you are encouraging an enormous turmoil in your breathing. Pause and let this turbulence surface. There may be yawning, sighing, or extra-deep breaths. After this phase subsides, feel how your breathing will settle again into a regular, even rhythm; a rhythm which, I am confident, will be much fuller, more satisfying, than before you moved your arm. After a while, roll over on your back or your stomach and do a comparison checkup before you continue on your other side.

Students tell me, after having done this experiment, that they feel as if their breaths were sweeping deep into their lower backs, or even into their pelvises.

This experiment will prove once again that not only your breathing but your whole body is under the influence of breathing work. You will be aware of increased circulation all through the body and of a change in muscle tone. When tired, do this experiment. It is a simple and sure way to recuperate and regain your energy.

If you emphasize the loosening up and settling down phase, you may also use this experiment as a means of falling asleep. Many students have successfully used it for this purpose, even under trying circumstances, both at the beginning of the night and after waking in the middle of the night.

V. A SPECIAL LEG MOVEMENT

Lying balanced on your side, with your knees pulled up in a comfortable position, one leg on top of the other, raise your upper knee ever so slightly, not lifting the foot (Figure 24). Hold your knee up for a moment, then let it return and rest again on the other leg.

Move extremely slowly and with the smallest effort possible. Feel yourself when moving. What, first of all, is the quality of your movement? What does it feel like? Moving so very slowly may make you notice that your movement began with an involuntary "startle" instead of slowly, as you had intended. You may become aware that it was jerky rather than steady, and that it was sometimes followed by collapse. Obviously, these are features of a poor way of moving. Try to overcome these malfunctions: aim for slow, gentle, steady, and flowing movements, executed with no more than appropriate effort. But even though your movements are not yet perfect, you will feel their stimulating effect on your breathing, as well as changes in your total bodily condition. You may yawn profusely, sigh with relief, draw fuller breaths, and feel your breathing spread vigorously through your trunk, particularly into the small of your back. At the same time you may feel the need to lengthen your trunk by wriggling so that you can rest solidly on the floor.

Do remain alert and responsive when you have turned over, and repeat the experiment on your other side. Be aware of whether your reactions are similar to or quite different from those when you were lying on the first side.

If you know beforehand that one side or one leg is in poorer condition than the other, use that one first. Later, having worked with your better side, or leg, return once more to the needy one, so that you give extra care to your weaker parts. Thus you avoid straining by using them each time for only a limited period.

Figure 24. Special leg movement.

21

The Awareness Experiment

By doing all the experiments so far described, you have trained yourself in the use of your body sense and have gathered experience in applying it in breathing work. You have developed a feeling for your breathing that now enables you to do a breathing experiment that relies especially on awareness and, of course, on yielding to needed change. The Awareness Experiment does not introduce, as the other breathing experiments did, external measures for breathing improvement, such as a tap, a stretch, or a sound. When doing the Awareness Experiment, you will be totally independent of locale, body position, and visible activity. Only your breathing matters; the aim is that you purposefully allow it to change in any way needed. For me, personally, the Awareness Experiment is the ultimate in breathing work.

Since you need time to work this experiment through successfully, you should plan for a long session each time and should spend a long time on each of its three phases.

Before you begin, do not forget the checkup, so that you can compare the state of your breathing at the beginning with its state at the end of your work session.

There are three phases in this experiment, corresponding to the three phases in your breathing. You can center your awareness on your exhalation, your inhalation, and on the pause between them.

The *first phase* is to try to *feel your exhalation*. Position is unimportant, provided you are comfortable. Work in many positions—sitting, lying, or moving. Your task is to become aware of your exhalations without interfering with them. Feel them again and again; accept whatever sensations may penetrate into your awareness. You may, at first, feel nothing in particular, or you may only become aware that you are disturbing your habitual way of breathing as soon as you try to become aware of your exhalations. Be patient; try to feel another, and yet another, exhalation. Gradually you will become aware of various features of your exhalations. Since each of us disturbs our breathing in different ways, I could not possibly predict what you as an individual might discover about your breathing. I can only urge you to keep an open mind to any sensations you may feel, and to give yourself all the time you may need to let sensations penetrate into your awareness.

There are a few helpful questions that you might ask yourself during the experiment: *"Do my exhalations happen on their own, or do I interfere with the process?"* "Do I tamper with the outflow of air, holding back or pushing air out?" Frequently you may find yourself behaving as if you did not really trust your own breathing to do the job of exhaling properly on its own. "Do I disturb my breathing by hurrying the exhalation, pressing on it or letting it flow only in spurts?" Our ways of disturbing are manifold, varying continuously. Once you have achieved a more precise awareness of one or more ways in which you interfere with your exhalation, try with each subsequent one to do it a bit less. Little by little you will feel that your exhalations come through more on their own. As you will become aware only gradually of the ways in which you disturb your breathing, this is a long process but a highly rewarding one. Even the least improvement will bring relief!

Next, ask yourself whether you are *giving your exhalations the full time they need*. "Do my exhalations last as long as they should?" You will find that they rarely do. You may well be cutting them short and for good reason—perhaps your schedule is very crowded or you are under considerable emotional pressure. If you sense that you are forcing your exhalations to end sooner than they would end on their own, try to let them terminate by themselves. You will need a long time to completely overcome such interference. Try to become aware of the ways you are interfering so that you can consciously try to be more "passive"; in this way, your exhalations will become less willful and more functional. Of course, with some breaths you will be more successful; with others, less. You may discover that your interfering has become habitual. All kinds of unexpected features that form these habits will penetrate into your awareness. However, interfering even only slightly less will have a calming effect and will make you feel better.

The *second phase* of the Awareness Experiment is to *become aware of your inhalation*. Again, you may have to cope with the problem of disturbing your breathing, this time your inhalations, as soon as you try to become aware of them. The earlier experience with your exhalations will undoubtedly make it easier for you to gain awareness and overcome such interference more quickly. Ask yourself what your inhalations are like. Do they flow on their own, or are you helping them along? Are you curtailing their length willfully, though unintentionally, before all the air has streamed in? Inhalations should be totally involuntary (a "gift of the gods," as I call them). Active help from you is an interference with this process. Take all the time you may need to become aware of the very personal ways in which you disturb your inhalations. Gradually you will experience a sense of great relief and deep satisfaction as your inhalations function more on their own, with less help from you.

The *third phase* of the Awareness Experiment is concerned with the *breathing pause*. Once again, feel your exhalations. Then try to become aware of how your exhalations change into inhalations. Feel whether, and in what ways, you interfere with the process. Try to sense what it is you do when interfering with the self-regulation of the transition. You may discover that you force your breathing instead of letting it happen spontaneously. You may hurry yourself, thereby cutting short the end of your exhalations and pushing your inhalations through before they are due. In this case, your inhalations begin willfully and too early, and the pause between exhalations and inhalations, the restful and preparatory period, is curtailed. When you interfere less with the transition, you will have the delightful experience of feeling the breathing pause as if it were "a wave rolling over the crest," as my students describe the sensation. This reestablishment of the full length of the pause, though it is only of short duration, is essential to a satisfying breathing rhythm.

The conscious experience of the rhythm, the constancy and effectiveness with which our breathing flows, will be a wonderfully gratifying experience. The Awareness Experiment will probably give you the greatest satisfaction of all. The fact that you provided no active stimulus but relied solely on the recuperative forces of your own breathing will give you a sense of trust in your breathing. A great feeling of relief accompanies the experience that one's breathing will take care of itself. You will feel ease and fullness in breathing that you may never have felt consciously, except for rare moments in your life. You will enjoy this quality of your breathing immensely. You will have a feeling of extreme physical well-being, calm, and serenity at the end of a work period. Your outlook on personal conflicts will have changed; you will feel strong enough to confront them and try to solve them. And finally, overflowing with new ideas, you will feel in full possession of the energy to pursue them, and be well equipped to cope with whatever difficulties may arise along the way.

22

Specifics for Emergencies

There are some everyday physical activities you would probably rather avoid doing, considering them either bothersome or strenuous. This is mainly because you do them without adequate support from your breathing. From time to time, you are probably equally stifled by emotional conflicts. All encumbrances, whether from physical or emotional stress, disturb your breathing. Any curtailment of your breathing will put you at a disadvantage in coping with a task or solving a problem. When conditions become highly critical, there is a tendency to forget experiences altogether (including breathing work!) that would enable you to help yourself. Use this chapter, "Specifics for Emergencies," to remind yourself what you are capable of doing through breathing work to make bodily tasks comfortable and emotional conflicts more bearable. You will find that as soon as you apply your skill to become aware of whether your breathing is supportive or constrained, you will always be reminded of a way to help yourself.

Shortness of Breath: This can be caused by physical exertions like running, climbing stairs, walking uphill, or by emotional distress. Recuperate fast by increasing your exhalations. Open your mouth and let the air stream out on *haaaa* (see Chapter 15).

Dizziness: Dizziness may be caused by bending over or straightening up. Unless it is caused by illness, you succumb to it only when you hold or squeeze your breathing while moving. Make sure not to hold your breath. As a precaution, let your exhalations out with a sound: *pfff* or *haaaa* (Chapter 15) or *ssss* (Chapter 14). Not hearing the sound brings the holding of your breath instantaneously to your attention and reminds you to let your breathing flow freely.

Heart Palpitations: Caused by poor breathing habits, palpitations can be overcome by prolonging exhalations. Every couple of breaths, open your mouth wide during an exhalation and let air stream out as freely as you can (see the Open Mouth Experiment, Chapter 13).

Feeling Chilly: Stimulate your breathing with tapping (Chapter 12) or letting air out on *ssss* (Chapter 14). As soon as your breathing becomes deeper, your circulation will increase and you will become warm all over.

Feeling Too Hot: Gentle breathing work has proved highly effective as a means of becoming comfortable during a heat wave. Try the Straw Experiment (Chapter 11). Exhalation through the open mouth (Chapter 13) is also advisable. Do either experiment for ten to fifteen minutes, and you will feel as if the heat wave had broken.

Hypertension as Well as Flabbiness: Level off to normal tone through breathing work. The most helpful experiments for these conditions are exhalation through a straw (Chapter 11); exhalation on *haaaa* on your palm (Chapter 15), or kneeling, head on the floor (Chapter 18), to overcome hypertension; tapping (Chapter 12) or exhalation on *ssss* (Chapter 14) to overcome flabbiness and restore your energy.

Childbirth: The help breathing can give is by now generally acknowledged and amply documented in the various books about natural childbirth.

Recovery from Anesthesia: When uncomfortable, use the exhalation on *haaa* (Chapter 15), and the open-mouth exhalation (Chapter 13). Even the exhalation on *ssss* (Chapter 14) has been useful.

Lack of Endurance and Slow Recuperation from Strain: These accompany inefficient breathing. Make sure that your breath is flowing freely, that you are not holding it or hampering it during and after bodily activities or emotional difficulties. This is the key to an almost limitless vitality that will enable you to cope successfully with emergencies. Choose any breathing experiment to which you have reacted particularly well. Emphasize your exhalations.

Lack of Sleep: This can be compensated for by taking care of your breathing. In a short time, experienced with breathing work as you are by now, you can get rid of waste gas, be replenished with oxygen, and then be capable of working for hours in a state of alertness and comfort. Use tapping (Chapter 12), exhalation through a straw (Chapter 11), exhalation on *ssss* (Chapter 14), or stretching (Chapter 20).

Trouble Falling Asleep: Take your favorite sleeping position and open your mouth ever so slightly when exhaling.* Do this for a number of consecutive breaths. Let the air flow out freely; do not force it. After you have achieved a couple of deeper breaths, your breathing will become regular and flow easily. This will bring desired sleep. Or use the special leg movement (described in Chapter 20). If you choose this experiment, emphasize the loosening-up and settling-down phase.

Sea and Air Sickness: These are avoidable as long as your breath flows unimpeded and is not held or made irregular. Consciously concentrate on your exhalations, making sure they are not stifled. Keeping your breaths flowing out and in rhythmically makes it impossible to pull your stomach up and hold it and yourself in a cramped position—one of the main causes of nausea. Use the exhalation on *ssss* (Chapter 14) or humming (Chapter 19). Both sounds need be barely audible, so as not to attract attention.

Balance: Whether standing, walking, or in the many extreme positions of the dancer, balance without strain is possible only if the breathing remains undisturbed. Once in a while, part your lips to let exhalations through. Part them just a bit, so little that it is hardly noticeable (see Chapter 13). This will achieve evenness of breath, which will support the balancing. Or use humming (Chapter 19).

* This is a variation of the Open Mouth Experiment (Chapter 13).

Carrying Packages: Carrying heavy or bulky packages, whose weight or odd shape disturb your customary way of standing or moving, will be strenuous if you interfere with your breathing. Letting your breath flow freely and evenly will ease the burden and avoid strain. Hiss (Chapter 14), hum on and off (Chapter 19), or exhale through your open mouth (Chapter 13) to keep your breathing flowing steadily and efficiently.

Pushing or Lifting Heavy Objects: These are the only activities in which holding your breath is an advantage. First, hold your breath; then, push or lift on the held breath. Take time between pushing or lifting to let your breathing become even. The muscles that do the main job need a solid base—your chest cage—from which to work proficiently.

Smoking and Overeating: When you want to *stop smoking* but feel an urge to smoke—which you will feel less the more you savor your breathing—do your favorite breathing experiment. If you are not alone and want to do the Straw Experiment, using a cigarette holder as a substitute for the straw will disguise your activity. Similarly, when the urge to eat too frequently tempts you, do a breathing experiment. It takes only three to five minutes, my students tell me, to overcome the desire for food. Though any experiment will do, it is best to use one that especially involves your mouth, like the Straw Experiment (Chapter 11), the Open Mouth Experiment (Chapter 13), or the Sibilant "S" Experiment (Chapter 14).

Headaches: Many disappear when you do breathing work. Any of the gentle experiments are helpful: the Straw Experiment (Chapter 11), the Open Mouth Experiment (Chapter 13), and the Skinfold Experiment (Chapter 16).

Depression: This is accompanied by shallow, feeble breathing. As soon as you induce your breathing to become stronger, your mood will change. Try the tapping experiments (Chapter 12); the pressure experiments, particularly Pressure on the Breastbone (Chapter 17); and the Exhalation on *ssss* (Chapter 14).

Overexcitement: So-called nervousness and general restlessness are always accompanied by a too-fast, too-superficial manner of breathing as well as by irregularities in breathing rhythm. Prolonging your exhalations will slow down your breathing and make it deeper. Interruptions of the rhythm will then fade away. Your emotional strain will ease along with the easing of your breathing. The Straw Experiment (Chapter 11), having an extremely calming effect, is especially helpful. Also do Exhalation on the Palm (Chapter 15) and the Open Mouth Experiment (Chapter 13).

Stage Fright: Stage fright overpowers you only as long as you leave your breathing in a disturbed state. Do a checkup on your breathing (see Chapter 10) and choose your favorite breathing experiment—the most appropriate one for overcoming your momentary disturbance. As soon as your breathing flows freely and rhythmically again, your stage fright will disappear. You will be in full possession of your skills, ready to perform.

Nervousness of Artists during the Waiting Time before Resuming a Performance: Instead of becoming restless and disturbed, use the time for breathing work. Any experiment will do. *Onstage:* Unobtrusively part your lips slightly on exhalation and let the air out as freely as you can without helping the process—a variation of the Open Mouth Experiment (Chapter 13)—or exhale almost inaudibly on *haaa*, as in the Exhalation on the Palm Experiment (Chapter 15). *Backstage:* Do any breathing experiments that you have found make your breathing fuller and freer. As your breathing recovers on its own once you have provided a stimulus, you will not be distracted from the performance.

Difficulties in Concentration and Poor Memory: Breathing experiments require your full attention. They force you to concentrate, thus training your mind not to wander. The experiences you have in a concentrated state are better remembered than those you have when your mind floats toward other subjects. The skill of concentration, once gained through breathing work, can be applied whenever and wherever needed.

Creative Blocks: In a state of held or interfered-with, irregular, or unsatisfactory breathing, ideas will flow sparingly and your productivity will be at its lowest. For any endeavor—in the arts, in business, or in personal relations—your spontaneity will be blocked. It will be released when your breathing functions without restraint. Choose whatever breathing experiment you may feel like doing.

Afterword

There is one last suggestion I would like to make. Now that you have read the book and tried the experiments, please reread the text again and again. As you continue to work, the words will gradually take on new meanings, different from those you perceived in them as a beginner. What at first glance may have seemed unimportant may become significant later on. You may even have misinterpreted my advice and done an experiment incorrectly.

And finally, let me answer as best I can the question that you will probably have asked yourself by now: "What will it really feel like when my breathing has changed for the better?" I would have to be a poet and not a teacher to answer this question properly. Instead, I would like to quote a student of mine who, when asked what her breathing change felt like, declared, "It was a glimpse of Paradise." It is my hope that you will achieve, through your own work, many equally delightful experiences.

Index

flabbiness (hypotension), *xvii*, 47
  emergency measures for, 114
forced breathing, *xxii*
  in Awareness Experiment, 110–111
  in Open Mouth Experiment, 60–61
  in Sibilant "S" Experiment, 62, 63
  in Straw Experiment, 46

Gindler, Elsa, *xxi*, *xxii*

headaches, 116
hearing, 94–96
heart, palpitations of, 114
heavy objects, pushing or lifting, 116
hiccups, 69–70
holding breath:
  as emergency measure, 116
  before movement, 98
hot feeling, emergency measures for, 114
"huddled up" breathing, 60
humidity, 14
Humming Experiment, 94–96
  as emergency measure, 115, 116
hunger sensations, 30
hypertension (overtension), *xvii*, 47
  emergency measures for, 114
hyperventilation, 24–25, 47
hypotension, *see* flabbiness

illness, 15
inhalation:
  in Awareness Experiment, 111
  increased, 47
  insufficient, 3, 21, 23
  in Open Mouth Experiment, 63
  during pressure experiments, 74, 76
  rhythm of, 12
intercostal muscles, 79–80
intercostal spaces, defined, 79
involuntary nervous system, *xix*

jaw, in Open Mouth Experiment, 59

Kallmeyer, Hede, *xxi*
kinesthetic sense, 8
kneeling, with trunk forward, 87–93
Kofler, Leo, *xxii*

leaning experiments, duration of, 84; *see also*
  position experiments
leg movement, special, 107, 115
leg stretch, 102–104
  on stomach, 104
lungs, *xviii*, 10
  tapping as stimulus for, 50–51, 54

MacKay, Steele, *xxi*
memory, poor, 117
movement experiments, 97–107
muscle tone, *see* tonus

nausea, 115
neck:
  in Open Mouth Experiment, 59
  in tapping experiments, 54
nervousness, emergency measures for, 117
nose:
  discharge from, 29–30
  in Open Mouth Experiment, 59–60
nostrils, widening of, 23

Open Mouth Experiment, 59–61, 62, 63
  as emergency measure, 113, 114, 116, 117
overeating, 116
overexcitement, 116–117
oxygen, *xviii*, 19, 24–25, 98

passive expansion, 82
pitch, Humming Experiment and, 95, 96
pneuma theory, *xxi*
pollution, *xvii*, 14–15
position experiments, 82–93
  as emergency measure, 114
positions, for breathing work, 32–33
pressure experiments, 66, 72–81
  areas for, 52–53
  as emergency measure, 116
Pressure on the Breastbone Experiment, 74–
  75, 116

rest position, 92
rib cage:
  elasticity of, 66, 72, 75, 76, 78
  lower front, skinfolds off, 68

rib cage (cont'd)
    pressure on, 76–81
    sides, skinfolds off, 69–70
ribs, pressure between, 79–81

Schlaffhorst, Clara, *xxii*
sea sickness, 115
shoulders, rising, 20–21
Sibilant "S" Experiment, 62–63
    as emergency measure, 114, 115, 116
sides, pressure on, 78
sighing, 21
sinuses, 29
skin, subcutaneous tissue underlying, 66
Skinfold Experiment, 66–71
    areas for, 52–53
    as emergency measure, 116
    partners for, 70
sleep:
    emergency measures for, 115
    lack of, 115
    tapping chest cage and, 56
smoking, 116
stage fright, 117
Stebbins, Genevieve, *xxi*
sternum, *see* breastbone
strain, recuperation from, 114–115
Straw Experiment, 44–49, 59, 62, 63
    for beginners, 61
    as emergency measure, 114, 115, 116, 117
    reactions to, 47
stretching, 22
    as emergency measure, 115

tapping:
    areas for, 52–53
    on breastbone, 57–58
    breathing responses to, 51–54, 56, 57–58

coughing caused by, 56
    as emergency measure, 114, 115
    experiments, 50–58
    hand positions for, 50, 57
    holding breath in, 51
    hunger sensations caused by, 30
    for muscle relaxing, in position experi-
        ments, 84, 87, 93
    reactions to, 51–54, 56, 57
    for relief of backaches, 29
    safe amount of, 73
    tenderness and, 56
temperature, for breathing work, 32
temperature changes, *xvii*, 14
tenderness:
    in pressure experiments, 73, 76, 77, 78
    in Skinfold Experiment, 69, 70, 71
    tapping as cause of, 56
throat:
    discharge from, 29–30
    in Exhalation on Palm Experiment, 64–65
    in Open Mouth Experiment, 59
tongue:
    in Open Mouth Experiment, 59
    in Sibilant "S" Experiment, 62
tonus, *xxii*, 20, 47–49, 106
trunk leaning sideways, 82–85

vocal cords, 94
voice, after Humming Experiment, 96
vowel sounds, in Humming Experiment, 95–
    96

weather conditions, 14
worry, *xvii*

yawning, 19–20